Housing Finance By Commercial Banks

Housing Finance By Commercial Banks

Dr. L. Rajani
Member of Faculty of Commerce
Department of Commerce
Yogi Vemana University
Kadapa

Prof. P. Mohan Reddy
Professor
Department of Commerce
S.V. University
Tirupati

SERIALS PUBLICATIONS
NEW DELHI (INDIA)

First Published – 2011

ISBN: 978-81-8387-436-6

Published by

SERIALS PUBLICATIONS
4830/24, 1st Floor, Ansari Road
Darya Ganj, New Delhi-110002 (India)
Phone : 23245225. Fax : 91-11-23272135
E-mail: serials@satyam.net.in

Dedicated to My Beloved Parents

SRI. LEVAKU. NARAYANA REDDY

&

SMT. LEVAKU. NARAYANA MMA

CONTENTS

FOREWORD

Housing is one of the bare necessities of human needs. Housing provides shelter for a family and it is said to be a total residential environment. It is not only an economic entity, but also offers social status and acceptance. Also it helps in urban growth, income distribution and the like. Improved location of dwelling in relation to jobs leads to reduction in traffic congestion and increased household take home pay by reducing commuting expenses. Housing finance in India was passive for long time and the neglect of government had a dampening effect on housing finance sector. The housing sector plays pivotal role in the economic development of the country. Housing finance has now been attracting a lot of attention in the country and the role of housing finance institutions in alleviating the housing problem in India has gained crucial importance. Today, almost all the financial institutions have entered this arena and competing with each other in providing housing loans at competitive interest rates. However, the entry of commercial banks into housing finance in a significant manner over the last few years has made many people to get aware of and avail the housing financial services to fulfill their long felt housing needs. The researcher has made a modest attempt in the present study to analyze the mobilization of funds by the sample borrowers, performance of select commercial banks in respect of housing finance, to identify the problems of housing finance faced by commercial banks and sample borrowers. I believe that the policy makers, bankers, researchers, post graduate students and users will find the study relevant in many ways.

Prof. C.Sivarami Reddy

Registrar, Yogi Vemana University, Kadapa

PREFACE

Food, clothing and shelter have always been considered basic human needs. Successive Indian governments have regarded housing as a primary need of the people. The need to provide affordable housing has been the reason behind State interventions in the sector. Housing policies, however, are usually framed by the governments from a social rather than economic perspective, since home life affects the very foundation of an individual's life, "Affordable Housing for All" is a national goal. The first step in house construction is collecting money to own a house. These days one need not have ready cash to start house construction. There are many financing institutions which give a helping hand in fulfilling one's dream of owning a house. Government of India and Reserve Bank of India have put in place a highly supportive policy framework for housing comprising fiscal incentives, monetary policy measures, administrative steps and other policies.

Housing finance as a specialist economic activity is of recent origin in India. It covers financing at all stages in the development of housing from purchase of land to construction and installation of on-site infrastructure. Housing finance sector offers safe and secure residential assets. good business opportunities for the lending agencies and attractive terms for the borrowers. The role of the commercial banks is particularly important in developing countries like India. The commercial banking system has been the largest mobiliser of household savings in the country. Today, not only the specialized finance companies but also commercial banks and cooperative banks are actively involved in housing finance. The commercial banks have established their separate housing finance institutions in the country.

Keeping this analysis, an attempt is made to analyse the nature and magnitude of problems confronted by the sample borrowers and at the same time by the sample commercial banks. The book provides a strong theoretical and analytical frame work and a consolidate picture of the four commercial banks. The study is comprehensively presented in seven chapters. The first Chapter covers a housing situation in India and the second Chapter reviews the housing finance system in India. The design and methodology of the study is included in the third Chapter. Chapters four analyze the performance of select commercial banks in India. Chapter five reveals the mobilization of funds by the sample borrowers. The problems of sample borrowers and select commercial banks are discussed in the sixth Chapter. The conclusions and suggestions are presented in the last Chapter. Suggestions, remarks and ideas expressed by distinguished experts have been incorporated by duly acknowledging the work. The present book may, therefore, aspires to be very useful to corporate managers, students, bank managers, users, researches and all those interested persons.

I owe a deep debt of gratitude to my research supervisor and co-author Prof. P. Mohan Reddy and his wife Smt. P. Shakeela, Department of Commerce, S.V. University, Tirupati for his valuable guidance in the conception and execution of this work. But for his constant encouragement and abiding interest in the project, I would have hardly completed it.

I am deeply indebted and grateful to Prof. C. Sivarami Reddy, and his wife

Smt. C. Reddamma, Register, Yogi Vemana University, Kadapa for his sympathetic interest and continuous encouragement in the progress of this project.

I owe my thanks to Prof. A. Ramachandra Reddy, Vice Chancellor, Y.V. University, Prof. L. Krishna Reddy (Rtd), Department of Chemistry and Former principal, Y.V. University, Kadapa and Prof. L. Nagamuni Reddy (Rtd),

Department of Mathematics and Former Rector, S.Y. University, Tirupati for their constant encouragement and help.

I would also to express my gratitude to Dr. S. Sudhakar Chetty, Principal, Govt. Degree College for women, Sri Kalahasti, Dr. G. Vijaya Bharati, Assistant Professor, Dept. of Commerce, Dr. Y. Subbarayudu, Assistance Professor, Dept. of HRM, Dr. P. Saritha, Assistant Professor, Department of MBA, Y.V. University, Kadapa and Dr. C. Subba Reddy, Lecturer in Commerce, S.K.R & S.K.R. Govt. College for Women, Kadapa for his expert view and suggestion from time to time on the work carried out by me.

My grateful thanks are due to the officials of State Bank of India, Andhra Bank, Syndicate Bank, Indian Banks and sample borrowers who have patiently and whole heartedly shared their time and provided useful information for his work.

I convey my deep sense of gratitude to my parents, to my husband C. Muralidhar Reddy, my daughter C. Hasini Reddy, mother-in-law, father-in-law, sister, brother, brother-in-law, sister-in-law, teachers, friends and other family members for their encouragement and help in writing this book.

Finally, I must thank serial publications for accepting my research work for publication.

L. Rajani

ABBREVATIONS

AB	–	Andhra Bank
ACHFS	–	Apex Co-operative Housing Finance Societies
ARDBs	–	Agricultural and Rural Development Banks
BPL	–	Below Poverty Line
CAGR	–	Compounded Annual Growth Rate
CGBS	–	Capital Gains Bonds Scheme
EMI	–	Equated Monthly Installment
ELNAR	–	Electronic Nostro Account Reconciliation
EWS	–	Economically Weaker Section
FCB	–	Foreign Commercial Banks
GDP	–	Gross Domestic Product
GFCF	–	Gross Fixed Capital Formation
GIC	–	General Insurance Corporation
GJRHFS	–	Golden Jubilee Rural Housing Finance Scheme
GOI	–	Government of India
HDFC	–	Housing Development Finance Corporation
HF	–	Housing Finance

HFC	–	Housing Finance Company
HFCs	–	Housing Finance Companies
HFS	–	Housing Finance System
HIG	–	High Income Group
HLAS	–	Home Loan Amount Scheme
HUDCO	–	Housing and Urban Development Corporation
IAY	–	Indira Awas Yojana
ICICI	–	Industrial Credit and Investment Corporation of India
IB	–	Indian Bank
IDBI	–	Industrial Development bank of India
IFC	–	International Finance Corporation
J&K	–	Jammu and Kashmir
LADS	–	Land Acquisition Development Scheme
LDSP	–	Land Development and shelter projects
LIC	–	Life Insurance Corporation of India
LICHFL	–	Life Insurance Corporation Housing Finance Limited
LIG	–	Low Income Group
NA.S	–	Nationalized Banks
NABARD	–	National Bank of Agriculture and Rural Development
NBFCs	–	Non-Banking Finance Companies
NBO	–	National Building Organisation
NCHF	–	National Co-opeartion Housing Federation of India
NHB	–	National Housing Bank

NHP	–	National Housing Policy
NHHP	–	National Housing and Habitat Policy
NPAs	–	Non-Performing Assets
NRI	–	Non-Residence Indians
NSS	–	National Sample Survey
OSCBs	–	Other Scheduled Commercial Banks
PCHFS	–	Primary Cooperative Housing Finance Societies
PHCF	–	Primary Housing Cooperative Federation
PLHS	–	Plantation Labour Housing Scheme
PLR	–	Primary Lending Rate
RBI	–	Reserve Bank of India
ROC	–	Return on Capital Employed
RHS	–	Rural Housing Scheme
RRBs	–	Regional Rural Banks
SB	–	Syndicate Bank
SBI	–	State Bank of India
STEP S	–	State Bank Electronic Payment Systems
SCBs	–	Select Commercial Banks
SCBBs	–	Select Commercial Bank Branches
UAs	–	Urban Areas
UTI	–	Unit Trust of India
ULCRA	–	Urban and Ceiling and Regulation on Act
VHS	–	Village Housing Scheme

Chapter–1

HOUSING SCENARIO IN INDIA

INTRODUCTION

Housing is one of the basic needs of society. A house is not only a place of dwelling but also an important social need of a family. It is observed that housing and quality of living are intimately related. Good housing also increases productivity of people. The life style of people including their culture are also reflected in the type of houses the people dwell[1]. A better house leads to a better standard of living, which in turn makes their life healthy and happy. Realizing the importance of housing in the national economy, institutional arrangements have been made during the recent past for the provision of housing finance in India.

Housing is a socio-economic aspect. Rural families use their houses as work places carrying on some economic activity. The poor give a low priority to housing compared to the rich. A house, like food and clothing is a fundamental need of human beings. The type of house in the beginning was controlled by natural factors and materials available in the nearby areas. Thus, "a house is a shelter and protection and provides for many the physical, biological, social and aesthetic processes, necessary to sustain life"[2]. Present concept, "a house is not simply a shelter but the right kind of shelter. It means provision of comfortable shelter and such surrounding and services as would keep it occupant fit and cheerful". Thus, it can be said that a house is an integral parts of modern society. House plays an important role in shaping the life-style of individuals and moulding the future of the society. In the present study, only those buildings as houses, which are used for residential purposes, i.e., living purpose are considered. Thus, buildings used for offices, schools and the like have not been considered as houses for assessing the magnitude of the housing problem. It is considered the housing shortage in various types of houses used for residence like pucca, semi-pucca, kutcha and the like.

Need for Housing

Shelter is a basic human need. It is the place which witnesses all the important events in the life of a human being. Indecent, unclean and inhuman living conditions seriously affect and endanger both the physical and mental health of individuals. For the progress of nation, it is essential that a confirming habitat in proper surroundings with minimum basic needs like drinking water and sewage are made available to every citizen. Housing demand of the other hand implies the tremendous increase of population in the country. Housing area per person continues to increase in certain nations and among the affluent segments of other nations, placing additional stress on prime space and building material[3]. The provision of housing as a social as well as merit good has been a challenging task, owing to a massive, need of investment, especially under the circumstances of underdeveloped finance system and the limited public investment on the part of the Government[4]. Thus, shelter has many connotations, which includes cost, choice, community and conservation aspects of house and its habitat.

Significance of Housing

Next to food and clothing, shelter is an essential ingredient of human life. House is not only a place of dwelling but also an important social need of a family.

- Housing is a place which builds mutual relationship among the family members and neighbours which, in-turn helps to build a clean and healthy society.

- The importance of housing in India has been gradually increasing and can be understood from its contribution to national income, its share in capital formation and employment generation.
- The importance of housing is revealed through the fact that even in the low-income families, after food, housing is typically the largest item of household expenditure[5].
- Housing is a package of services, land, public facilities and access to jobs.
- One of the basic requirements besides food and clothing, the national policy is to progressively reduce or eliminate the existing housing shortage over a certain period of time
- Proper housing is necessary in a community, if level of health is to remain high. Bad dwellings also lead to deterioration of health of their unfortunate inmaters[6].

HOUSING IN INDIA

Housing is an important component and measures the socio-economic status of the people. It is regarded as a critical sector in terms of policy initiatives and interventions. The relevance of housing as a social need is long recognized and has, therefore, influenced the policy making at different levels viz., national, state and local levels. This is reflected in the efforts of the Government that has undertaken to improve the housing and habitat conditions by way of financial allocations in the Five Year Plans and Union Budgets[7]. The Government of India has also been adopting several measures to encourage NRI investment in housing and real estate development for promoting the flow of foreign exchange to the country. The Working Group on Urban Housing for the 9th plan gave a thrust to housing development and targeted construction of 8.87million units.

The National Housing and Habitat Policy 1998 emphasizes "Housing for All" by the end of 2007 together with services, social infrastructure, strong public-private partnerships and the role of the co-operative and corporate sector[8]. Thus, there will be a massive flow of funds to the housing sector in the days ahead and with the ever increasing encouragement from the Government of India, the housing sector of the country remains poised for a spectacular growth acting as a catalyst in the growth of the economy, a powerful engine of economic development. On the other hand, in a developing country like India the augmentation of housing units are not kept in pace with the demand in the country. This problem is commonly seen in urban areas and more over the migrants from rural areas belonging to low income groups are more affected with this problem. At the present pace of growth, urban centers will face chaotic conditions for housing provision and the shabby image of our cities will create questions over environmental sustainability of human settlements. To ameliorate housing conditions in slums, radical changes are required in the present land policies assuring tenure security. However, by and large government strategies on slum relocation or redevelopment have failed. Furthermore, it was recognized that the private sector housing market excludes a large segment of population below the poverty line in the urban centers due to limited profitability. This implies that there is a need for a reorientation in the present notions of housing provision by public intervention, which becomes an urgent need to provide housing for all.

Population Growth in India

Population explosion is one of the main factors for creating the housing shortage and indecent housing in India. The uncontrolled growth of population and urbanization has affected the overall of well-being of the people as the family life thereby affecting the national development. According to 2001 census, India had a total population of 1027 million, which makes India, the second largest country in the world in terms of population size after China. The population of the country has grown steadily over the past decades.

Table 1 (Chart 1) represents the rural and urban population in India. The total population of India during 1931-1941 was 319 million, of which the urban population was 44 million

Table 1
Population Growth in India

(in million)

Year	Population: Rural	Population: Urban	Total	Urban Population as Percentage of Total Population
1931-1941	275(86)	44(14)	319(100)	13.8
1941-1951	299(83)	62(17)	361(100)	17.2
1951-1961	360(82)	79(18)	439(100)	18.0
1961-1971	439(80)	109(20)	548(100)	19.9
1971-1981*	524(77)	159(23)	683(100)	23.3
1981-1991**	628(74)	218(26)	846(100)	25.7
1991-2001	741(72)	285(28)	1027(100)	27.8
2001-2011 ..	834(69)	360(31)	1194(100)	30.15
2011-2021 ..	950(66)	468(34)	1417(100)	33.03

Note: Figures in parentheses of total population

* includes projected population of Assam where 1981 census was not conducted

** includes projected population of Jammu & Kashmir where 1991 Census was not conducted

.. Estimated projections of Census of India 2001

Sources :

1. National Housing Bank Reports, New Delhi : 2005-06.
2. e-CENSUSINDIA - No.3 of 2001, New Delhi: 30, Oct. 2001.

Chart 1: Population Growth in India

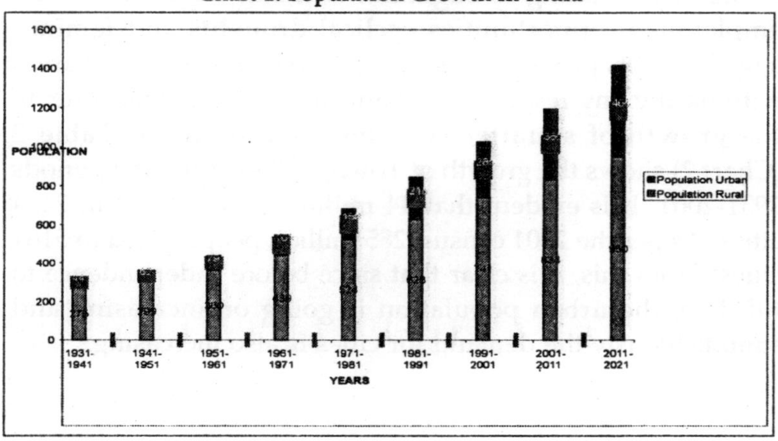

constituting 13.9 per cent in total population. It was also seen that there was an abnormal increase in the total population by 1991-2001. Of the total increase of 1027 million in both urban and rural population, the share of urban and rural areas are 741 and 285 millions respectively. The percentage of urban population increased by as large as 27.8 per cent. It is also observed that there was a tremendous increase in the percentage of urban population when compared to that of rural population in the successive five decades viz, from 1931-1941 to 1991-2001. The increasing urban population naturally leads to more demand for housing units in the urban areas of the country. The urban population is expected to increase to 468 million and the total population to 1417 million by the year 2021. The rate of growth of the urban population in the total population will be 33.03 per cent in 2021 decade[9].

Growth of Urban Agglomerations and Towns / UAs

One of the peculiarities of economic growth in India has been the fair dispersal of population between the rural and urban areas. Urbanization in India is not due to large-scale industrialization but due to the inability of rural areas to provide viable employment opportunities as a result of population growth within the sector leading to marginalization of holdings. Disguised employment and unemployment become more pronounced leading to migration to urban centres for better employment opportunities cyclical droughts and famines aggravate this problem when people come in from rural areas with hardly any resources. Urbanization of this kind leads to the growth of squatter settlements and slums. Table 2 (Chart 2) shows the growth of Town/ UAs during the periods 1931-2001. It is evident that 44 million people lived in 2424 cities. As per the 2001 census, 285 million people lived in 5161 cities. From this, it is clear that since before Independence to till date, the urban population is going on increasing and simultaneously the demand for cities is also increasing.

Table 2
Growth of Urban Agglomerations and Towns / UAs

(in number)

Years	*Urban*	*No. of Towns/UAs*
1931-41	44	2424
1941-51	62	3060
1951-61	79	2700
1961-71	109	3126
1971-81*	159	3949
1981-91**	218	4615
1991-2001	285	5161

Note:
* includes projected population of Assam where 1981 census was not conducted
**includes projected population of Jammu & Kashmir where 1991 Census was not conducted
Source: National Building Organisation–Hand Book of housing statistics, Part I, New Delhi:2001.

Chart 2: Growth of Urban Agglomerations and Towns/UAs During 1931-2001

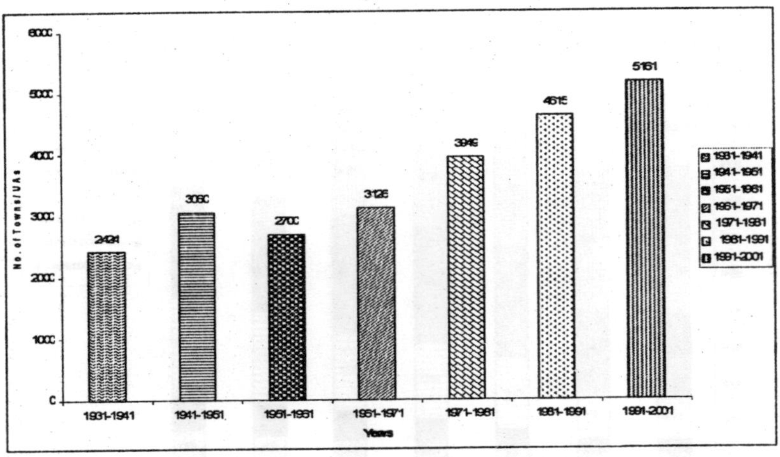

Growth of Urban Towns by Size Class during 1931-2001

Table 3 (Chart-3) shows the Urban Agglomerations and Towns by class/category of cities from 1931-1941 to 1991-2001. It is clear by evident that the number of total towns/UAs gradually increased from 2424 in 1931-1941 to 5161 by 1991-2001.

Table 3
Growth of Urban Towns by Size Class During 1931-2001

(in number)

Year	*Total Towns/ UAs*	*Size of Class*					
		Class I 100000 & above	*Class II 50000-99999*	*Class III 20000-49999*	*Class IV 10000-19999*	*Class V 5000-9999*	*Class VI Less than 5000*
1931-41	2424	52	88	273	554	979	478
1941-51	3060	76	111	374	675	1195	629
1951-61	2700	107	139	518	820	848	268
1961-71	3126	151	219	652	988	820	296
1971-81*	3949	226	325	883	1247	920	348
1981-91**	4615	322	421	1161	1451	973	287
1991-01	5161	441	496	1388	1561	1041	234

Note:

* includes projected population of Assam where 1981 census was not conducted.

** includes projected population of Jammu & Kashmir where1991 Census was not conducted

Source: National Building Organization - Hand Book of housing statistics, Part I, New Delhi: 2001.

Chart 3: Growth of Urban Towns by Size Class During 1931-2001

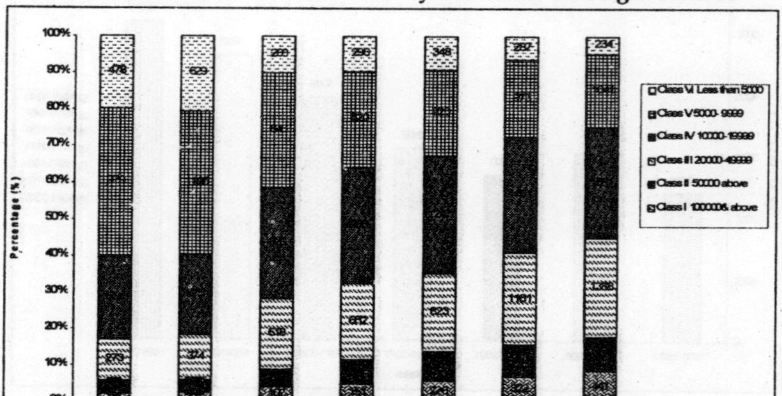

Of these, cities with more than one million population increased by more than twelve fold during the period. The total urban population is accomplished in 52 class I cities with a population of one lakh or above in the years 1931-1941, which

gradually increased to 441 by 1991–2001. The number of towns with a population ranging between 50000 and one lakh which is generally referred to as class II cities are 88 in the year 1931-9141 and increased to 496 by 1991-2001. It is observed that the population of class III cities which possess population between 20000-49999 are in 273 in 1931-1941 and increased to 1388 by 1991-2001.

Similarly, the populations of class IV and class V cities with a population between 10000-19999 and 5000–9999 are 554 and 979 respectively during 1931-1941, which gradually increased to 1561 and 1041 respectively by the year 1991-2001. The last category i.e. class VI cites marked a distinct variation. The numbers of class VI cities which possess a population of less than 5000 range were 478 during 1931-1941 and decreased drastically to 234 by 1991-2001. Thus, it is clear that while there was constant increase in the number of larger urban centres (class I to V), the number of smallest urban centres (class VI) decreased phenomenally between 1931 and 2001. This may be due to increasing migrations towards larger cities in search of employment opportunities.

Growth of Metropolitan Cities

The industrialization and trade expansion have given rise to the establishment of towns and mini-cities or urban agglomerations in the country. As these cities are the major source of employment and contributors to the national economy and productivity, there is need for proper infrastructural development, which should be inspired with the philosophy of economic and social development. The mega cities in India are fast assuming eminence because of their continuous growth both inwards and outwards. The mega cities are both centers of production and consumption and hence, they attract workers, employees, entrepreneurs, professionals and managerial, software and technical personnel.

Table 4 shows the Growth of Metropolitan Cities in the total urban population during 1941-2001. It may be noticed that there is remarkable growth in the number of cities during

Table 4
Growth of Metropolitan Cities in the Total Urban Population During 1941- 2001

Year	*No.of Metropolitan Cities*	*Population (in million)*	*Share in Total Urban Population Percentage (%)*
1941	02	5.31	12.23
1951	05	11.75	18.81
1961	07	18.10	22.93
1971	09	27.83	25.51
1981	12	42.12	26.41
1991	23	70.66	32.54
2001	35	108.34	37.87

Source: National Building Organisation –Hand Book of Housing Statistics, Part I,New Delhi: 2001.

Chart 4: Growth of Metropolitan Cities in the Total Urban Population During 1941-2001

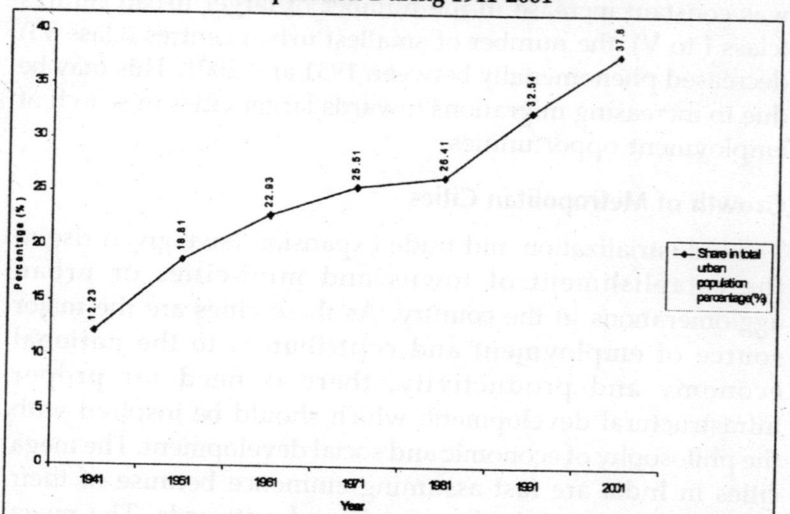

the period. In 1941 India had only tow metro cities with a population of 5.31 million and their share in total urban population percentage was 12.23, while in 2001, there were 35 such cities with a population of 108.34 million and their share in the total urban population per cent was 37.87. There is an abnormal growth of these cities from 1981 to 1991, form 12 to

23 cities. Chart 4 represents the growth of metropolitan cities in the total urban population. The National Commission on Urbanization has described urbanization in India as processes where by the surplus population of workers from rural areas resettle in urban centers where non-agricultural job opportunities are available. If job opportunities are productive and lead to gainful employment, urbanization will becomes a catalyst for economic development. If, however, urbanization is merely a process of transfer of rural poverty to an urban environment, it results in a concentration of misery. Describing the civic conditions in urban areas, the commission pointed out that the urban centers in the country, generated the most brutal and inhuman living conditions, with large sections of the population living in squatter settlements. Overcrowding and scarcity of water and sanitation results in severe health problems and degradation of human life. The commission estimated that there would be 468 million people living in urban areas in India by 2021 compared to 285 million in 2001. Urbanization, according to the Commission, has been accelerated by distress migration from rural areas.

Housing Contribution to Gross Domestic Product (GDP)

Housing contributes to Gross Domestic Product (GDP) in two ways: through private residential investment and consumption spending on housing services. Consumption spending on housing services includes the amount of rent paid by tenants, the computed value of housing services to homeowners, and the amount paid to hostels by households for housing services.

The share of housing in GDP and Gross Fixed Capital Formation (GFCF) would go up substantially in the next coming years. Outstanding housing loan as a percentage of GDP has raised from 3.4 per cent 2001 to 7.25 per cent in 2005 and 8.50 per cent in 2006. The figure had pegged at about 9 per cent is far less than China with 10 per cent, European Union and USA with 40 per cent and 60 per cent respectively. In view of the increased investment in the service sector, this contributes about 50 per cent to the nation's GDP, and growth in urbanization.

PROBLEMS OF HOUSING

In India, housing is necessity shading into a luxury. Its supply does not fully meet the present needs of the Indian population, whether in terms of location, size, tenure, type or facilities due to inadequate attention have been paid to this important sector.

- The problem of housing is universal. But it is much more acute in a developing country like India. Despite quantitative increase in housing over successive plan periods, the housing situation in India continues to be daunting and deplorable. The imbalance between demand and supply in housing has been a matter of deep concern both for the Government as well as for the planners of India [10].
- The task of achieving the goal of "Shelter for all" is a gigantic one. In India, the housing situation differs widely from state to state and region to region, while the housing problem in rural areas by and large is qualitative in nature, the problem in urban area is largely quantitative.
- Charles Abrams, stated that mankind has made unprecedented progress during the 20th century in the realm of industry, education and science but most of the human race still does not have a simple shelter providing privacy and protection[11].
- In expanding housing facilities, during the past two or three years, the main problems which have arisen and to which attention has to be given are the following :
  - In rapidly growing towns, developed cities are not available to a sufficient extent. Construction in the private sector tends to concentrate on expensive houses intended to fetch high rates and the requirements of the lower, middle and middle classes are not adequately catered for;
  - Apart from assistance which the government now provides, adequate institutional arrangements for housing finance do not exist;

- Cooperative housing has made comparatively little progress;
- There is considerable need for research in building materials and techniques and for prescribing standards of construction with due regard to the availability of local materials and the economic use of scarce material ;
- With a few exceptions, State Governments are not yet adequately organized for undertaking and assisting extensive housing programmes;
- The major problem of the housing sector is inadequate funds. The available funds are not sufficient to meet the growing needs of the housing sector; and
- The problems in rural housing are many and varied. The fluctuations in the incomes of rural households, difficulty in assessing the repaying capacity of the rural borrowers, non- availability of title deeds, are impediments in financing rural houses. Even the operational costs of finance institutions in rural areas are very high. It is also a problem that the institutions operations in rural areas perceive higher risk with rural housing credit.

Measures like reduction in stamp duty and registration charges and development of the infrastructure for health, education and the like will have significant bearing on the development in rural areas. A uniform model of housing finance will also facilitate the finance institutions to lend easily and there by enhance the flow of credit to this sector.

Population Households and Residential Housing in India

Growth in population, formation of new households and residential occupied residential houses are inter related factors. The income of a households plays a vital role in house building activities and in determing the housing characteristics-especially on quantitative aspects. The housing situation in

India today is highly dynamic due to the decline in the household size coupled with increase in income. Table 5 reveals the population, households, housing stock and persons per house in different census years.

It may be observed therein that the average number of persons per house in urban areas has declined continuously from 6.06 in 1951 to 5.50 in 2001. On the contrary; the scenario in the rural sector has been somewhat fluctuating. The figure was 5.52 in 1951, which increased to 6.03 in 1981, but declined to 5.50 in 2001. Occupancy i.e., the number of persons per house, in both the urban and rural areas became almost equal by 2001. The decennial growth rates of urban and rural population have shown a decaling trend during the past decades, 1981-1991 and 1991-2001.

The growth rates of housing stock and household formation in the past two decades have more or less followed the same declining trend of population growth in urban areas. However, in the rural areas, the growth rate of housing stock increased during 1991-2001. The decline in growth rate of housing stock coupled with the increase in growth of household formation accounts for increase in housing shortage in rural areas.

Condition of Housing

The condition of housing structures over the last fifty-year period has witnessed significant improvement. The total number of pucca houses, which were only 18.8 per cent of the total occupied houses in 1961, had gone up significantly to a level of 51.65 per cent in 2001. As a result, the percentage of katcha houses, which was 44.6 per cent in 1961, ha fallen to 18.2 per cent in 2001. The trend in the increasing percentage of pucca houses, semi pucca houses and katcha houses, in the total occupied houses during the improvement in the housing condition over the last 40 years. And the semi pucca house, which was 36 per cent in 1961, has fallen to 30 per cent in 2001. In absolute terms the number of pucca houses in rural areas has increased from 33.4 million units in 1991 to 47.48 million by the year 2001. This implies that use of permanent building

Table 5

Population, Households, Residential Housing Stock, Persons Per House Holds and Person Per House 1951-2001

Census year	*Population (In millions)*			*Households (In millions)*			*Occupied residential houses (In millions)*			*Persons per houses (In per cent)*		
	Urban	*Rural*	*Total*	*Urban*	*Rural*	*Total*	*Urban*	*Rural*	*Total*	*Urban*	*Rural*	*Total*
1951	62.4	298.50	360.90	12.8	60.6	73.40	10.3	54.10	64.40	6.06	5.52	5.60
1961	79.10	360.10	438.20	14.9	68.6	83.50	14.0	62.2	79.20	5.65	5.79	5.55
1971	108.90	438.30	547.20	19.10	78.0	97.10	18.10	72.7	90.80	6.02	6.03	6.03
1981	159.70	525.50	685.20	29.10	93.5	122.60	27.20	87.2	114.40	5.87	6.03	5.99
1991	217.61	628.70	846.31	40.74	112.66	153.40	39.40	109.00	148.40	5.52	5.77	5.70
2001	286.12	742.49	1028.61	53.69	138.27	191.96	52.06	135.10	187.16	5.50	5.70	5.50

Sources: Report on Trend and Progress of Housing in India–National Housing Bank–New Delhi: June 2004,P.60.

materials for the construction of walls and roof is becoming more popular in rural areas also. The average annual housing completions in urban areas per 1000 population was around 7 housing units during the last three decades (1971-81 to 1991-2001). However Government programmes like Indira Awas Yojna and rural house–site and construction assistance schemes for rural landless workers and artisans have contributed to improved housing situation.

Housing Shortage in India during 1961-2001

Housing shortage, in a statistical sense, is to be calculated on the basis of number of houses and households. It can also be conceived as a measure of inadequacy or otherwise, of the existing provision in the light of a "socially acceptable norm". Hence, housing shortage is a gap between the total demand and the total stock of houses. Housing shortage may arise owing to many reasons. The trend of population growth, internal and external movement of population, changes in families and household structures, lack of supply of sufficient number of residential units because of scarcity of financial and material resources and the like are the most obvious reasons.

Housing shortage in India was first recognized during World War II, especially after 1947 when about 7.5 million displaced persons migrated to India, in the wake of partition of the country. As mentioned earlier, exponential growth of population coupled with nuclearisation of families resulted not only in pressure on the existing available houses but also growing requirements of additional houses[12]. The imbalanced regional growth has also led to increased pressure on the urban centers due to migration of population from rural to urban agglomerations resulted in the increasing number of slums and squatter settlements. Table 6 depicts the housing shortage in India.

The shortage was 15.2 million units in 1961. The shortage including congestion is to be 41 million units in 2001. This is based on the assumption that household formation and additions to housing stock will grow at the same rate as in the

Table 6
Housing Shortage in India During 1961-2001

Years	*Housing Shortage (In millions)*
1961	15.2
1971	14.6
1981	23.3
1991	31.0
2001	41.0

Source:
1. Census of India 2001.
2. National Building Organisation, the Hand Book of Housing Statistics Part I, New Delhi:2001.

past. On the whole the average shortage in housing units increased. This is because of the shortage of funds and inadequacy of financial institutions, coupled with an increase in building material, labour and loan costs.

Households and Number of Rooms

Both in the urban and rural areas, the number of households living in one room has shown a decling trend during the last four decades, whereas, an increasing trend is seen in the other categories i.e., one room, two rooms, three rooms and more than three rooms.

Table 7 displayed distribution of households by size or dwelling units occupied. The size of houses has increased in the case of urban areas as compared to the rural areas.

As per census 2001, the condition of the urban residential houses is better than that of the rural areas. The households residing in houses without least one room decreased 45.8 per cent to 35.1 per cent and 44.3 per cent to 38.5 per cent in urban and rural households in decades 1981-2001. Between 1981 and 2001, both in urban and rural areas, while proportion of households occupying single room declined, the consequent improvement was reflected in the two rooms, three rooms and above three rooms. This leads to the interference that bigger houses have come into being during the period.

Table 7

Distribution of Households by Size of Dwelling Units Occupied from 1981-2001 Censu

(in percentage)

	Rural			*Urban*			*Total*		
No.of Rooms	*1981*	*1991*	*2001*	*1981*	*1991*	*2001*	*1981*	*1991*	*2001*
One room	44.3	40.8	38.5	45.8	39.5	35.1	44.7	40.5	38.5
Two room	28.9	30.6	30.0	27.8	30.4	30.4	28.4	30.6	30.0
Three room	12.2	13.5	13.3	12.2	14.8	14.8	12.2	13.8	14.4
More than Three	14.6	15.0	16.8	14.4	15.3	15.0	14.4	15.1	17.2

Sources:

1. Census of India 2001
2. Report on Trend and Progress of Housing in India, National Housing Building, New Delhi : June 2004,P.10

Housing by Tenure Status

The tenurial status of the households can be classified into two categories viz., 'owned' and 'rented'. The tendency to own a house has shown an increasing trend among urban households. The distribution of households living in owned and rented houses in rural areas is shown in Table 8.

Table 8
Tenure Status in Urban and Rural Areas

(in percentage)

Tenure Status	*1961*	*1971*	*1981*	*1991*	*2001*
Urban					
Owned	46.2	47.1	53.5	65.9	71.5
Rented	53.2	52.9	46.5	34.1	28.5
Rural					
Owned	93.6	93.8	93.0	94.5	95.4
Rented	6.4	6.2	7.0	5.5	4.6

Source :
1. Census of India 2001
2. Report on Trend and Progress of Housing in India, NHB, New Delhi: June 2004,P.11

It can be observed that is marginal decline in rural households residing in rented houses from 6.4 per cent in 1961 to 4.6 per cent by 2001. The rural households residing in owned houses increased from 1.8 per cent varied between 1961 and 2001. But, the proportion of rural owner households has, however, declined marginally from 93.8 per cent to 93.00 per cent during 1971-81. The corresponding increase in households rental housing in rural areas presumably reflects the demand arising form the opening of schools, banks, primary health centres and the like in rural area.

It is further observed that the percentage of urban households residing in own houses increased to 46.2 per cent in 1961 from 71.5 per cent in 2001. This was due to the establishment of HUDCO and HDFC during this period which concentrated more on urban areas.

PLAN ALLOCATIONS FOR HOUSING ACTIVITY

Under the Indian Constitution, though housing is a state subject, the assistance for housing is provided jointly by the Central and State Governments in view of huge size of the problem. The Central Government has introduced a number of Social Housing Schemes and concentrated more on the advisory service. The State and Union Territories have been vested with full powers to execute the housing projects.

First Five Year Plan (1951-56)

The Central Government took this housing subject to develop it through plans. Therefore a responsible place for housing has been found in the plan outlays. During the Five First year plan an independent Ministry of Works and Housing has been designed and in 1954 the NBO (National Building Organisation) was created particularly to design low-cost housing.

Second Five Year Plan (1956-61)

The Second Five Year Plan has witnessed a healthy progress in the housing field. Public finance institutions like the LIC, made a breakthrough, in the housing activity in India. Many more schemes like Plantation Labour Housing Scheme (PLHS), Village Housing Scheme (VHS), Land Acquisition and Development Scheme (LADS), Housing Schemes for Scheduled Castes and Scheduled Tribes were launched to support the specific needs of certain sections of the society. The Central Government started indirect financing system for the housing through State Governments.

Third Five Year Plan (1961-1966)

The Third Five Year Plan has made provision for the formulation of as many as 400 Master Plans for the establishment of Urban Centres (medium and large) in the country. This plan has specified the need for land acquisition, and the control of real estate market. It was towards the end of this plan many housing boards came up particularly to eliminate housing shortage for Low Income Group (LIG) and slum categories. On the other hand, city level organizations like Development, Authorities, Urban Improvement Trusts, Slum Clearance Boards (SCB) were established by many states.

Fourth Five Year Plan (1969-74)

The Fourth Five Year Plan envisaged the idea of strengthening housing programmes by establishing public housing agencies and resultantly the HUDCO was established in 1970, to fight the housing problem comprehensively. The HUDCO was instituted with the objective of providing long term finances for construction of houses, undertaking urban development programmes and infrastructure facilities. Almost all the states have completed the formalities of establishing housing boards, city level authorities and metropolitan centers by the mid-seventies. The budgets of the State Governments, the LIC and the HUDCO also supported them.

Fifth Five Year Plan (1974-79)

The Fifth Five Year plan admitted various constraints and limitations and lacuna in the housing system. The analysis set out the feeling that it is extremely difficult for any developing country heading towards development with all social ideals to implement such ambitious housing programmes.

Yet another significant development that came up in this plan period was the establishment of private sector financial institution viz., the HDFC (Housing Development Finance Corporation) in 1977, which has come to the rescue of the individuals, co-operative societies and corporates by providing them financial assistance.

Six and Seventh Five Year Plans (1980-85 and 1985-1990)

During the Sixth and Seventh Five Year Plans, the role of public housing agencies was given a high priority. A very big achievement of this plan period could be attributed to the creation of the National Housing Bank in 1988. The RBI with an idea of co-ordinating the multifarious housing activities by various agencies have created an apex body the NHB. The total dimension of housing scenario has changed ever since the advent of the NHB.

The National Housing Policy (NHP) was launched on May 12, 1988. It aims at eradication of "houselessness" by the turn of the century by not only wiping out the existing backlog of housing needs but also by enabling the additional households to secure for themselves housing at least as per the minimum housing norms[13].

The basic objectives of the national housing policy

- making available developed land at reasonable rates for housing;
- providing security of tenure to households both in the rural and urban areas;
- creating an environment conducive to investments in housing for rental purpose
- making available standards impetus to co-operative and group housing activities as well as institutionalizing and curbing luxury housing.
- undertaking steps to initiate financial support to the selected groups.

The NHP's contribution, to the field of housing finance, is quite outstanding especially for bringing in a sort of discipline, co-ordinated control over the entire housing system of the country. NHP has integrated all sources of housing finance to direct the overall picture of housing development[14].

Eighth Five Year Plan (1992-97)

At the beginning of the Eighth Five Year Plan, the housing scene had dominated of the private activity. The plan emphasized the intervention of the state in a big way particularly with reference to the majority of vulnerable sections who are by and large neglected by private agencies. Highlighting the urgency of housing development, the world has declared 1987 as the international year of the shelter for the homeless, which promoted speedy progress on the housing front.

Ninth Five Year Plan (1997-2002)

At the onset of the Ninth Five Year plan, Indira Awas Yojana (IAY) is the most important rural housing scheme. The National Housing Policy (NHP) 1994 was to provide access to adequate "Shelter for all". There was an enormous shortage in the housing sector due to major deficiencies in the housing related to infrastructure. Government has since adopted a new Housing and Habitat Policy, which was approved by the Cabinet in July 1998. The National Housing and Habitat Policy (NHHP) enunciated in 1998 had envisioned eradication of houselessness, improvement in housing conditions of the inadequately housing people and providing a minimum level of basic services and amenities to all. The central theme of the policy was to enable strong public-private partnerships for tackling housing and infrastructure related problems[15]. The Housing and Habitat Policy aims a housing finance are listed below[16].

- to facilitate up-gradation of infrastructure of towns and cities and to make these comparable to the need of the times;
- housing finance institutions will take up the task of attracting resources from provident funds, insurance funds and mutual funds;
- facilitating accelerated supply of serviced land and housing with particular focus to economic weaker section and low income group categories and taking into account the need for development of supporting infrastructure and basic services to all categories;
- facilitating restructuring and empowering the institutions at state and local governments to mobilize land and planning and financing for housing and basic amenities;
- establishment of a Management Information System in the housing sector to strengthen monitoring of building activity in the country;
- development of cities and towns in a manner which provide for a healthy environment , increased use of

renewable energy sources and pollution free atmosphere with a concern for solid waste disposal, drainage and the like.

Tenth Five Year Plan (2002-07)

The Tenth Five Year Plan was to promote a balanced and equitable regional development and to advance the necessary policy and administrative reforms at the state level. The allocation for 2003-04 includes several additional initiatives such as promoting infrastructure by leveraging public money through private sector partnership, provision of hand-pumps in water scarce areas and schools, rejuvenation of traditional water sources in villages, research and development support in pharmaceuticals, wind and solar energy, among others. The major task is to evolve market friendly reforms relating to tax and infrastructure to help in increasing investment flow in housing. Emphasis has been laid on need to supply affordable housing to Economic Weaker Section (EWS) and LIG through proper programme of allocation of land, extension of funding assistance and provision of support services. Rationalization of stamp duty was also being done in phases to bring it down to no more than 5 per cent by the end of the Tenth plan period[17]. The centrally sponsored Valmiki Ambedkar Awas Yojana (VAMBAY) was introduced in 2001 with a view to enhancing the housing conditions of the urban slum dwellers living below the poverty line without adequate shelter[18].

Eleventh Five Year Plan (2007-2012)

The Eleventh Five Year Plan period i.e., 2007-2012 will be estimated by the Working Group on Urban Housing Requirements and Ministry of Rural Developments, Government of India. It has been estimated that 26.53 million additional houses requirement in urban areas during the plan of which more than 90 per cent will be for the poor, i.e the EWS, and LIG segments with estimated fund requirements about Rs. 5401crores.

The Ministry of Rural Development, Government of India has estimated housing requirement of 47.43 million housing units in rural areas during the Eleventh Plan period of which more than 80 per cent is envisaged for below the poverty line (BPL) families.

SITUATIONS IN INDIAN HOUSING

India's population has already crossed the 1 billion mark and it is estimated that by the year 2021, 350 million people will be added with further concentration of population in urban centers upto 12 per cent. According to Census of 2001, India had a total residential housing stock of 187 million with only 51 per cent permanent dwelling units. Furthermore, out of this housing stock 54 per cent have no sanitation facility. The lack of basic infrastructure facilities in the present housing stock and the shortfall indicates chronic shortage of dwelling units with basic needs. Moreover, it is estimated that by the year 2021 the population of urban poor will be nearly 180 million.

This indicates that at the present pace of growth, urban centers will face chaotic conditions for housing provision and the deplorable image of our cities will raise questions over environmental sustainability of human settlements. To ameliorate housing conditions in deteriorating slums, radical changes are required in the present land policies assuring tenure security. However, by and large government strategies on slum relocation or redevelopment have failed. Furthermore, it was recognized that the private sector housing market excludes a large segment of population under the poverty line in the urban centers due to limited profitability. This implies that there is a need for a reorientation in the present notions of housing provision by public intervention, which becomes an urgent need to provide housing for all.

According to an estimate, India had a chronic shortage of 21.23 million dwelling units, out of which 36 per cent are required in urban centers. The Ninth Five-Year plan suggests that there is a need to build/upgrade 10 million dwelling units for urban poor or EWS and 5 million for LIG in the urban centers alone. Considering the present rate of supply of urban housing, the future rate of supply has to be accelerated three times to eradicate the housing problem in urban areas.

However, it seems to be difficult for public sector agencies to accelerate rate of housing provision looking at the limited financial resources of Rs. 34,000 crore in comparison to the required investment of Rs. 1,21,370 crore for urban centers.

The present crisis in the housing sector and dilapidated living condition of LIG and EWS segments are largely due to inappropriate government interventions. Although, Government has used various strategies to fulfill the housing demand, the current state of affairs indicates an alarming level of backlog in affordable housing especially in the LIG and EWS segments. This, along with an ever increasing shortfall, leads to exponential growth in housing demand. To eradicate housing shortage, the National Housing and Habitat Policy (1998) aimed at providing shelter to all by 2010, but this seems to be a dream rather than a reality[19].

REFERENCES

1. Housing Development: An overview, Chennai: The Hindu, Aug 2006, p.1.
2. Editorial, Mumbai: Yojana, Dec, 1976, pp.15-31.
3. Lakshmi Narasaiah, M., Protection growth and housing, National UGC Seminar, Department of Commerce, Government College for Men, Puttur, Aug 2006, p.3.
4. Mahadeva, M. and Thera Bhai–Housing Finance: Can Commercial Banks Meet People Housing Finance Needs? Vol 34, No.1, Oct-Dec 2001, p.57.
5. Seventh Five Year Plan, 1985-90, New Delhi: Government of India, pp.22-23.
6. Report on Trend and Progress of Housing in India, New Delhi: National Housing Bank, June 2005, p.3.
7. Petter, D.F., Cardozo., Housing -Engine of Economic Growth, Managing Director, Mumbai: AN FIN HOME Ltd, 2006, p.1.
8. NIUA Urban, Hand book 2000, New Delhi: National Institute of Urban Affairs, January 2000, p.1.
9. Economic Survey of Delhi 1999-2000, New Delhi: Planning Department, March 2000, pp.13-14.
10. Braja Bandhu Padhiari and Prakash Chandra Mirsa, Rural Housing Finance, New Delhi: DiscoveryPublishing House,2004, Vol-XV, p.218.

11. Suresh, V., Basket of Options by HUDCO for Housing Co-operatives, 11th Souvenir, New Delhi: NCHF, 1995, p.6.

12. Mahadeva, M., Housing Finance Portfolio of Scheduled Commercial Banks (SCBs), Tend Analysis 2000-05, Occasional Paper No.1, New Delhi: National Housing Bank,May 2007, p.4.

13. Report on Trend and Progress of Housing in India, New Delhi: National Housing Bank, June 1992, p.4.

14. Government of Indian Draft National Housing Policy, New Delhi: Ministry of Urban Development, 1987, pp.12-13.

15. National Housing and Habitat Policy, New Delhi: Government of India, 2007, pp.10-12.

16. www.NHHP.com.in

17. National Housing Bank, New Delhi: Annual Reports, 2002-03, pp.15-16.

18. Reports on Trend and Progress of Housing in India, June 2004, National Housing Bank, New Delhi: p.17.

19. Hetal H. Patel, Effectiveness of housing and Habitat Policy, LSA-UK, Real Estate Developer, Ahmedabad: Center for Environmental Planning & Technology (CEPT) 2005, pp.3-4.

CHAPTER–2

HOUSING FINANCE SYSTEM IN INDIA

INTRODUCTION

Housing is a significant engine for growth and development of the economy. Housing constitutes an important component and a measure of the socio-economic status of people. It is a critical sector for the India's growth. Housing finance is a specialist economic activity of recent origin in India. It was completely neglected in the past, but with many players entering the market in recent years, the competition in the housing finance sector has increased tremendously. The huge demands for housing has propelled housing finance firms engage the price wars. The Government initiatives are also making this sector one of the economic growth drivers for India. Housing is a sunrise industry with a gap between demand and supply[1]. The present boom in the housing sector is set to provide a platform for the housing finance companies to carve out a fortune[2]. According to Wallace F. Smith "*Housing Finance is a factor of production quite distinct from labour, materials and risk taking*"[3].

Due to the high competition in the housing finance industry, the lending rates are at an all-time low and the lenders are offering attractive packages to customers. The Housing finance companies also got a share from the proposed change in the 1999-2000 budgets in the tax treatment of income earned on non-performing assets and the assessment of tax on interest on loans on an accrual basis rather than on an actual basis, corporate bodies can avail of 40 per cent depreciation (earlier 20 per cent) on new dwelling units purchased by then for their employees, this will encourage them to invest in housing for their employees.

Affordable housing is generally defined as decent, quality housing that costs not more than 30 per cent of household's gross monthly income for rent/mortgage and utility payments. In the present scenario, people susceptible to low or irregular income are likely to find it difficult to buy their own house. Moreover, the rapid increase in house prices and rents in urban centres have pushed the dreams of owing a house beyond the reach of a growing number of Low Income Group (LIG) and Economic Weaker Sections (EWS).

It is estimated that the housing finance sector will grow by 24.1 per cent over the next five years[4]. Recognizing the growing need for housing finance in India, the Government has emphasized the importance of housing and housing finance in its Ninth Five Year Plan. This is the first time that India has emphasized the importance of the housing sector that there is a short fall of more than 20 million units. It is also estimated that the housing finance by banks will go up by 50 per cent. That means a lower return on the capital of banks, unless they increase their lending rates[5].

Nature of Housing Finance

The housing finance sector still has a long way to go before it can serve all sections of the population who are not part of the formal sector, who do not have regular income and whose spending power is low. Housing finance is easily available only in the large cities, not in towns and villages where the majority of the population still lives. Besides, the security, collateral and other legal requirements to avail housing loans, prevent large sections of the population form getting access to institutional funds for housing. The housing finance companies generally sanction upto 85 per cent of the value of the property, but the limit varies among companies. The balance will have to be put in by the buyer.

Need for Housing Finance

On an average a person lives almost two-thirds of his life on a house, therefore, access to a safe, secure, durable and healthy shelter becomes absolutely necessary. As per an estimate by the National Building organization (2001), nearly 75 per cent lived in an inadequate shelter out of which 48 per cent were below the poverty line[6]. The price of owning a house or flat is increasing day by day. In such circumstances, people have no option other than to live in rented apartments. However, wise people go for housing finance. Through the Housing Finance System, people benefit in that they can have the pride of owning the house provided their monthly installments are with in their financial limits. The lower and middle class people can at large benefit from this Housing Finance System. The Housing finance in India has become one of the most popular techniques used by people to purchase or construct a house. Union Finance Minister *P. Chindanbaram* announced a package of measures in budget 2006-07 to encourage corporate bodies and institutional investment in housing[7].

Housing-A Neglected Social Sector

An affordable shelter embodies the values of the users and forms an integral component of the fabric of neighborhood life as well as the entire social milieu. Shelter, thus, has many connotations, which includes cost, choice, community and conservation aspects of a house and its habitat. In the context, the Pre-Independence housing in India was influenced by British imperial philosophy of town planning, which neglected the Low Income Group (LIG) and Economically Weaker Sections (EWS). After Independence, India's policies have become more democratic, socialistic and republic, which has represented the public sector's image as grossly inefficient to provide shelter to all. However, the interventions of neo-liberalized economist have resulted in realization of the potential role of the private sector in housing provision. However, it took a long time to emerge with a platform for private sector's entry into the affordable housing market in an efficient and practical way.

Need for Reforms

Housing has been one of the prime concerns of the Indian Government through all its Five Year Plans. The role of the public sector in housing provision was framed in the First Five Year Plan– "The private enterprise is not in a position to do the job so far as the low income groups are concerned. They cannot afford to pay an economic rent for housing accommodation of even the minimum standards". With this conception, Government adopted mass housing strategies for slum dwellers and other target groups with highly subsidized houses during the 1960s .However, to a large extent, benefits of these efforts were limited to certain target groups, and it was only a drop in the ocean. During the 1970s, many aspects of public housing were recognized and radical changes were adopted to reform land policies in order to provide housing finance, improving environment of slums by providing better environment, infrastructure and social amenities rather than slums clearance.

The emerging institutions were urban development authorities, Housing and Urban Development Corporation (HUDCO) and Housing Development Finance Corporation (HDFC). However, the setting up of these institutions has hardly helped the urban poor. With the intention to help the urban poor, government enacted the Urban Land Ceiling and Regulation Act (ULCRA) in 1976, which aimed to pass on the surplus land to the urban poor. Despite its wide objectives, very recently the act has been re-enacted because of its failure at large. The only significant change in this decade was the introduction of site and service schemes and self-help housing with tenure rights, which also contributed but only meagerly to the total housing demand. By 1980s Government started realizing that with the limited resources, it could not address the mammoth housing problem and a strong need was felt for private-sector participation. The Five Year Plans state that the Government should be involved in housing "not so much to build but to promote housing activity".

This way the gradual shift in the role of Government from initiator to facilitator was realized and the first generation of reforms were initiated during 1991 by evolving public-private partnership mechanisms of housing provision to achieve efficiency and effectiveness. After 1991 the first generation of reforms began, which increased private sectors investment in housing and had direct implications on the Gross Domestic product (GDP).

INDIAN HOUSING FINANCIAL SYSTEM

Independence, the Indian financial system has over the period, expanded rapidly and at the same time experienced reasonable stability. It should be pointed out that at the time of Independence, India's financial system was rather small although both savings and investment rates were not so low, being respectively around 10 per cent and 11 per cent of the

Fig. 1: The Housing Finance Organization Structure in India

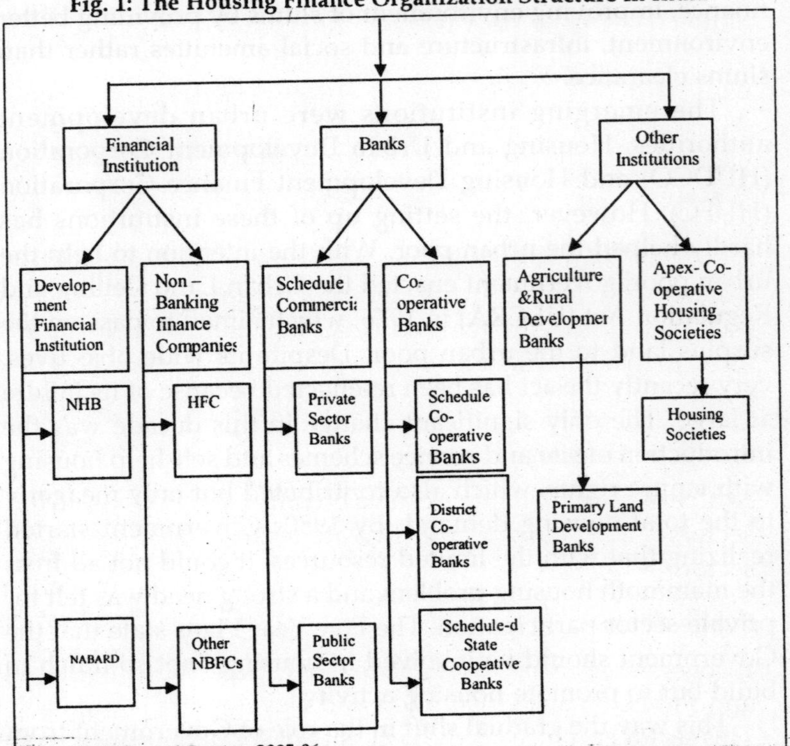

Note: NHB Annual Report- 2005-06

Gross Domestic Product (GDP). Most investment was made by through individuals savings directly with only a small portion of savings through financial institutions. The Housing Finance Organization Structure in India shown in the figure 2.1[8]. An organized institutional housing finance system was lacking. Informal agencies have played a significant role in financing the housing activity. The Last six decades have seen significant institutional development in the area of housing finance in our country. India has now a national level public Sector institution, Housing and Urban Development Corporation (HUDCO), was established in 1970 and catering to all income groups in an integrated and financially viable composition. In the private sector, the Housing Finance Development Corporation (HDFC) was established in 1977 and it is the first primary housing such as LIC,GIC and commercial banks have institution catering to individual loan requirements. There are also moves to set up more HDFC type institutions in the country.

HFIs have been increasing in number both in the public as well as in the private sector. In addition to the housing development, finance is extended as a part of governmental regulation on investment patterns. Institutions established specialized housing finance subsidiaries to undertake direct household mortgage loan operations. The National Housing Bank has been set up by the government of India with the primary role of mobilizing deposits required for the housing sector through local saving and loan associations. Deliberations also are in an advanced stage to promote a separate company to take on the job of introducing mortgage insurance in India.

Source of Housing Finance

Source of housing finance can be broadly categorised into three sectors Viz., Public sector, Private sector and Co-operative sector.

Public Sector

It covers the central Govt., State Govt., State Housing Boards, and Public Finance Institution and Development Authorities. This sector emphasizes the necessity of social housing schemes beneficial to the poorest sectors. The contribution of this sector is very small.

Private Sector

This sector is represented by builders, developers and private housing development agencies. Contribution of household savings is also a significant source in this sector. This sector caters to the needs of higher-income and upper-middle income groups.

Co–operative Sector

This sector is represented by the housing co-operatives, the district and central co-operative banks, and urban Co-operative banks. Among these, housing co-operatives, which have been formed mostly by the economically weaker sections, low-income and middle-income groups play a significant role. They are being supported and assisted by the Government and the people themselves.

The High Level Group set up by the Government of India in June 1986, under the chairmanship of Dr. C. Rangarajan, the then Deputy Governor, RBI, has adopted yet another classification of sources of housing finance Viz. formal and informal.

According to this group, the formal sector includes

- Budgetary allocations of central and state governments.
- Financial institutions like GIC, LIC, UTI, Commercial Banks and Provident Fund organizations.
- Specialized housing finance institutions Viz. HUDCO, Apex and Primary co-operative housing finance societies and
- Housing finance companies like HDFC.

Co-operative Housing Societies and Housing Finance

The British East India Company miserably exploited India by absorbing all its resources during the pre-Independence period. After independence, earnest steps were taken to make the country healthy in every respect. It was generally admitted by the architects of India that co-operatives can act as an effective media for the economic reconstruction of the country. Hence attempts were made by the planning commission to develop the co-operative movement as a self reliant one, by augmenting the resources through mobilization of savings in urban and rural areas, promoting integrated rural development by strengthening the links between credit, supply of inputs, processing, marketing and distribution of essential commodities and developing the weaker section of the community.

The concept of the co-operatives as an institutional mechanism for satisfying various needs of the people is premised on the principles of 'self-help' as well as 'collective effort' Housing co-operatives have a prominent place in the co-operative movement in the country. During the year 2005, it is estimated that there were over 92,000 primary housing co-operatives with over 6.5 million members.

The co-operative sector has played an important role in providing housing to its members and has made a significant impact across the country. The co-operative sector is expected to play a lead role, particularly in land acquisition, allotment of land and housing sites to encourage group housing and the development of amenities in their projects, as envisaged in the National Housing and Habitat Policy.

The National Co-operative Housing Federation of India (NCHF) is a nation wide organization of the Indian Co-operative Housing Movement. It was founded in September 1969 by the Apex Co-operative Housing Federations. The basic thrust of its formation was to have an organization at the national level to assume the responsibility of promoting, developing and coordinating the activities of housing co-operatives in the country. The NCHF operates through 26 apex cooperative housing federations in the states. There are nearly 90,000 primary cooperative housing societies with 6.5 million individual members.

NCHFI Objectives

The objectives of NCHFI are :

- to promote a common forum for dealing with technical, financial and practical problems relating to housing co-operatives and to devise ways and means of solving them;
- to raise funds by borrowing or otherwise;
- to grant loans or advances to members;
- to promote apex co-operative housing federations in those states where such an organization do not exist;
- to procure, manufacture, stock and supply building material to housing co-operatives and the general public;

The co-operative housing structure consists of primary housing co-operatives at the grass root level and Apex Co-operative Housing Federations (ACHFs) at the state level. ACHFS at the state level are affiliated to NCHF, with their growth strategies, policy formulations and evolving housing programmes besides inter facing with various institutions to channel finances for these federations for onward lending to competitive borrowers. In addition, NCHF also helps the ACHFS in improving this financial, organizational and technical capabilities[9].

The rest of the Co-operatives are:

- those that get finances from other sources;
- those that have not get started construction activities; and
- those which have repaid their loans fully.

These ACHFS have so far disbursed Rs 9,182.25 crores to primary housing Co-operatives for construction of dwelling units for their members. The co-operatives in turn have constructed 2.30 million houses.

Mobilization of Resources

The share in total borrowing from LIC has shown a declining trend and stood at 38.38 percent. It has decreased from 46.4

per cent in 2000-01 to 40.5 per cent in 2003-04. Though borrowings from HUDCO have been approximately Rs.1500 crores during the last three years, its share in total borrowings had depicted a marginal decline from about 22.5 per cent in 2000-01 to 17.96 per cent in 2004-05. The share of banks and State Government in the total borrowings had been increasing in the past five years which suddenly plunged in 2004-05 to 2.13 per cent. The shares of deposits, which have been nominal in the past years, have increased significantly to 23.37 per cent in outstanding cumulative borrowings during the year. Over the period 2000-01 to 2004-05, the contribution of the NHB to total borrowings by ACHFs has increased marginally from about 8.5 per cent to 9.59 per cent. The average loan per dwelling unit for all ACHFs was about Rs.0.69 lakhs during 2004-05. The quantum of cumulative sanction of housing loans by the ACHFs increased to Rs.9, 601.8 crores during 2004-05 while cumulative disbursal rose to Rs.9,182.40 crores. Cumulatively the financial assistance provided by ACHFs till March 31, 2004 enabled construction of 2.30 million dwelling units[10].

Housing and Urban Development Corporation (HUDCO)

Urban Development Corporation (HUDCO) was set up on April 25th, 1970 in the public sector. It is a limited company, fully owned organization of the Government of India. HUDCO is a specialized financial institution to fund state Government, their specialized agencies, like housing boards, urban development corporations and municipal bodies for their urban infrastructure projects[11]. But ever since it has entered the individual housing finance sector, the entire scenario has changed. The main change was in interest rates that had actually begun when HUDCO had started giving housing finance for 11.5 per cent and the interest rates come down to 8.81 per cent. HUDCO has been financing urban infrastructure projects in water and sewage, roads, area development and housing in a big way. The present paid up share capital of HUDCO is Rs.2001.90 crores and in addition as reserve and surplus of Rs.1672.32 crores (as on 31.12.06). HUDCO was instituted with the objective of providing long-term finance for construction, housing undertaking urban development programmes and infrastructure facilities.

HUDCO's assistance covers the housing needs of all income categories of the society mainly Economic-Low Income Groups and High Income Groups. It also assisted extensively in the provision/rehabilitation of service, drainage, solid waste disposal, road network, socio-cultural infrastructures buildings for health, education and recreation and shopping and marketing facilities and also provides loans for construction of hostels for working women. HUDCO has played a major role in the implementation of the National Housing Policy (NHP). It has been entrusted with the implementation of the priority programmes of the ministry like, low cost sanitation, night shelter for footpath dwellers, shelter up gradation under Nehru Rozgar Yojana, and the rural housing and urban minimum needs programme[12].

Objectives of HUDCO

The objectives of HUDCO are outlined as follows:

- to finance and undertake housing and urban development programmes in the country;
- to finance or undertake wholly or partially in setting up of new industrial towns;
- to subscribe to the debentures and bonds to be issued by the state Housing and urban Development Boards, Improvement Trusts and Development Authorities;
- to administer the money received from time to time from the Government of India and other sources as grants or otherwise for the purpose of financing or undertaking housing and urban development programmes in the country;
- to organize housing and urban development programmes in India with special emphasis on low cost housing;
- to develop of new townships and their infrastructural needs;

- to facilitate consultancy services within India and abroad;

Role of HUDCO in Housing

As on 31.01.2007, HUDCO contributed to the construction of over 141.44 lakhs dwelling units including up-gradation of 41.29 lakhs units all over the country. Of these, while 86.21 lakhs houses benefit the rural housing needs, as the balance 55.23 lakhs the urban housing needs. HUDCO has so far sanctioned 14379 projects (excluding Urban Infrastructure projects) involving a total amount of Rs.27616 crores. About 55 per cent of housing loan of HUDCO has been allocated for Economically Weaker Sections (EWS) and Low Income Group (LIG) which carries a concessional rate of interest of 8.5 per cent (floating) to 9.75 per cent (floating). Over 95 per cent of the dwelling units sanctioned by HUDCO benefit these sections of society. In the last 36 years, HUDCO has reached people in over 1799 towns and hundreds of villages. Much of the assistance is project oriented ensuring that the housing is affordable, technically sound, financially viable, legally acceptable and above all environmentally appropriate.

Housing Development Finance Corporation

Housing Development Finance Corporation (HDFC) was often described as an extraordinary company, run for ordinary Indians. It was India's premier Housing Finance Company and one of the most successful and most admired financial institutions in the country. HDFC had done well in a business that no other business group in the country had thought of venturing into. Even as the housing finance market looked increasingly crowded in early 2000. HDFCs business model was robust.

History of HDFC

Husmukhbhai Parekh incorporated HDFC as a public limited company on 17th October 1977[13]. In 1976, after his retirement from ICICI, he put together a blue print for a housing finance bank. On recognizing the need for a specialist housing finance institution in the country, he decided to venture into the resource intensive and unexploited area of business. He first convinced the government about the need for an institution solely for provisioning housing finance in the country. As a result of his committed efforts, HDFC was established in 1977. The Company's mandate was to provide housing finance to individuals, co-operative societies and the corporate sector. Its equity capital was subscribed by the Indian Business Community (Rs.45mn), an Indian public Issue (Rs.40mn), Industrial Credit and Investment Corporation of India (ICICI) (Rs.5mn), International agencies like the International Finance Corporation (IFC), Washington (Rs.5mn), an affiliate of the World Bank also subscribed to the equity of HDFC. The IFC also provided a loan of US $ 4 million in the beginning to HDFC. And through public issue it could collect Rs.10 crores in the beginning. Thus, the concept of specialist housing finance institutions was well received by the Government, international agencies, financial institutions and public. But its low share of equity ensured that the fledging organization had sufficient independence. Hasmukhbhai's towering stature also helped in minimizing interference. It aims at promoting 'home ownership'. HDFC provides various schemes like home savings plan, home loans, home improvement loans, short term bridging loans and loans under NRI scheme. The HDFC normally provides the loan for a period of 5 to 15 years. The repayment period is not be, ordinarily, extended beyond the age of retirement of the borrower or his/her reaching 65 years of age, whichever is earlier. The repayment is equated in monthly installments comprising principal and interest.

HDFC Bank has increased the interest rates on NRI and FCNR Deposits with immediate effect. HDFC bank has increased NRI term deposits rate to 6.43 per cent for one to less than three years. On FCNR dollar deposits of one to less than two years, it has raised the rate of 5.42 per cent[14]. Almost 90 per cent of initial shareholding was in the hands of domestic institutions and retail investors. In 2005, 78 per cent of share hold was by foreign institutional investors. In 2005, HDFC bank won Asia money's Best domestic commercial bank award[15].

Mobilizing Resources

Rising of mobilizing resource was the main challenge. Apart from equity capital, HDFC raises loans from IFC, ICICI, LIC, GIC, UTI and banks. It also mobilizes funds from the public in the form of deposits. It introduced the Certificate of Deposit (HDFC-CD) scheme in 1979 for larger deposits and Loan Linked Deposit' (HDFC-LLD) scheme to attract the deposits from the smaller households. The HDFC-LLD scheme has encouraged small savers to deposit in multiples of Rs.100 with HDFC. In the year 1984-85 HDFC also introduced another scheme called House Savings Plan(HSP), which is similar to the Home Loan Account Scheme(HLAs) of National Housing Bank. The minimum savings period to make a borrower eligible for loan under the scheme is 25 months. The only source of money for providing finance under the scheme is the savings accumulated by the potential borrowers. The raised through this scheme are kept separate from these funds is restricted only to the members of the scheme. The specialty of this scheme is that the member is eligible for a house loan at a predetermined rate of interest. Usually, the rate of interest for house loans under this scheme would be at a lower level when compared to the normal house loans sanctioned by the organization. The capital structure of HDFC is shown in Table 1.

Table 1
Debt Equity Ratio of HDFC

Year	*Debt Funds (Rs. in crores)*	*Equity Funds (Rs. in crores)*	*Total Funds (Rs. in crores)*	*Debt/equity Ratio (in times)*
1999-2K	12988.54	2095.97	15084.51	6.20:1
2000-01	15469.78	2371.94	17841.71	6.52:1
2001-02	18755.69	2702.84	21458.53	6.94:1
2002-03	23252.28	3043.86	26296.14	7.64:1
2003-04	28684.04	3393.79	32077.83	8.45:1
2004-05	36647.40	3883.10	40530.50	9.43:1
2005-06	46721.35	4468.33	51189.68	10.46:1
2006-07	57193.03	5551.40	62744.43	10.30:1
2007-08	69151.22	11947.34	81098.56	5.79:1

Source: Compiled from HDFC's Annual Reports

This Table 1 describes the Debt funds (long term debts + deposits), Equity funds (equity shares + reserves) and Debt/ Equity Ratio. The housing finance institutions during the period from 1999-2k to 2008-09 mobilizing resources in the form of long term borrowed funds and public deposits. This has made its capital structure highly generated. The Debt/ Equity Ratio 6.20:1 times in the year 1999-2k at the time the capital adequacy ratio for 14.5 percent. In the year of 2004-05 the Debt/Equity Ratio rise has 6.38:1 times, the capital adequacy ratio is a rounded form 13.4 percent. Equity funds as a proportion of total assets increased from 20 percent to 36% and bonds, debentures and commercial papers 32 percent. However, made the capital formation of HDFC more balanced.

Chart 1: Debt Equity Ratio of HDFC

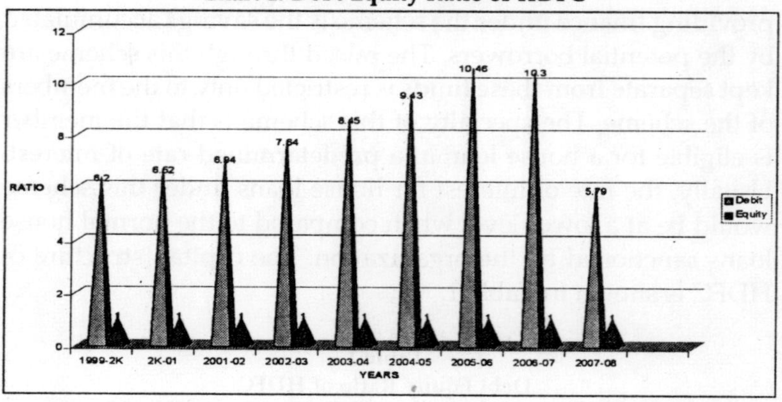

Operational Performance

Table 2 presents the approvals, disbursements and percentage of disbursements and approvals.

In the year 1999-2k the total approvals Rs 5305.15 crores and the total disbursements Rs. 4492.74crores, the percentage 84.7. In the year 2004-05 the approvals has rise Rs.49166.00 crores and disbursements Rs.39650.00 crores it formed 84.65 percent. Finally the approvals improved and also the disbursements increased but conclude that disbursement has reduced that time operational performance satisfactory.

Table 2
Housing Approvals and Disburesements by HDFC

Year	*Approvals (Rs. in crores)*	*Disbursements (Rs. in crores)*	*Total*	*Percentage of Disbursements to Approvals*
1999-2K	5305.15	4492.74	9797.89	84.7
2K-01	6879.77	5801.01	12680.78	84.3
2001-02	9041.25	7616.56	16657.81	84.2
2002-03	11731.57	9950.87	21682.44	84.8
2003-04	15215.56	12696.82	27912.38	84.4
2004-05	19715.33	16206.75	35922.08	84.2
2005-06	25633.67	20679.20	46312.87	80.7
2006-07	33331.93	26177.99	59509.92	78.54
2007-08	42520.00	32874.99	75394.99	77.34

Source: Complied from the Annual Reports of HDFC

Chart 2: Housing Approvals and Disbursements by HDFC

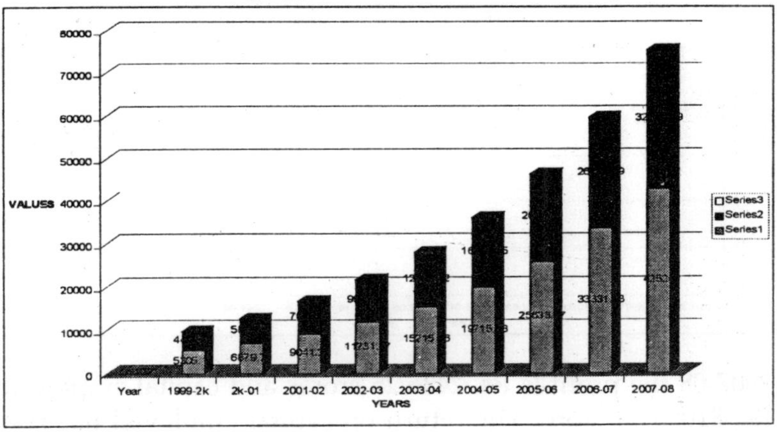

Profitability Performance

Profitability of a business is an important variable to judge the efficiency and viability of a commercial enterprise. The profitability indicators viz return on capital employed and return on net worth for hopes are shown in the following Table 3 and Table 4.

In the year 1999-2k the profit after tax and capital employed is rounded Rs. 401.81 crores and Rs. 15084.51 crores respectively. The compared between capitals employed and profit after tax the return on capital employed 2.66 percent. As compared with

Table 3
Return on Capital Employed of HDFC

(Rs. in crores)

Year	*Profit After Tax*	*Capital Employed*	*Ratio (%)*
1999-2K	401.81	15084.51	2.66
2000-01	473.65	17841.71	2.65
2001-02	580.00	21458.53	2.70
2002-03	690.29	26296.14	2.63
2003-04	851.78	32077.50	2.66
2004-05	1036.59	40530.50	2.56
2005-06	1257.30	51189.68	2.46
2006-07	1570.38	62744.43	2.50
2007-08	2436.25	81098.56	3.00

Source: Complied from the Annual Reports of HDFC

Chart 3: Return on Capital Employed

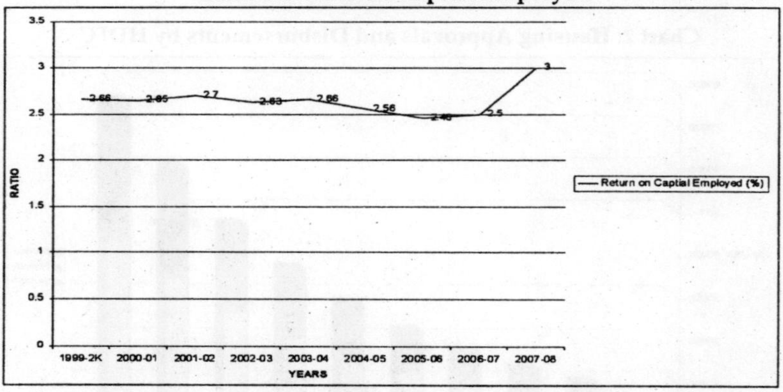

2007-08 the profit is Rs. 2436.25 crores and capital employed Rs. 81098.56 crore. The return on capital employed has rise percentage is 3.00. The return on capital employed is low margin commercial activity.

Table 4
Return on Net Worth of HDFC

(Rs. in crores)

Year	*Profit After Tax (Rs. in crores)*	*Net worth (Rs. in crores)*	*Ratio (%)*
1999-2K	401.81	2095.97	19.17
2000-01	473.65	2371.94	19.97
2001-02	580.00	2702.84	21.46

Contd.

Year	*Profit After Tax (Rs. in crores)*	*Net worth (Rs. in crores)*	*Ratio (%)*
2002-03	690.29	3043.86	22.68
2003-04	851.78	3393.79	25.10
2004-05	1036.59	3883.10	26.69
2005-06	1257.30	4468.33	28.14
2006-07	1570.38	5551.40	28.29
2007-08	2436.25	11947.34	20.39

Source: Complied from the Annual Reports of HDFC

Chart 4: Return on Net Worth

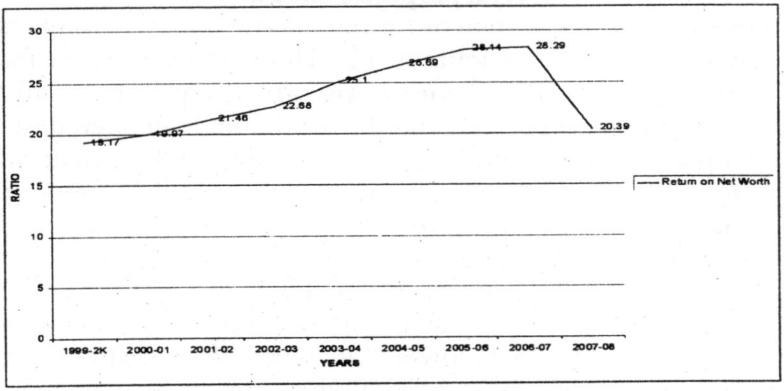

Table 4 describes the return on net worth includes profit after tax and net worth. Net worth includes shareholder funds and reserves. The profit after tax has Rs. 401.81 crores and net worth Rs. 2095.97 crores. The net worth is 19.17 percent. As against the profit after tax Rs. 2436.25 crores and net worth of Rs. 11947.34 crores is increased and the return on net wroth rise in 20.34 percent. The analysis of net profit of net wroth percentage indicates that HDFC's performance is maximizing the wealth of the organization.

Insurance Corporations and Housing Finance

The Life Insurance Corporation Housing Finance Limited (LIC) as well as General Insurance Corporation of India (GIC) support housing activity both directly and indirectly. Life Insurance Corporation Housing Finance Limited (LICHFL) is one of the largest housing finance companies in India having one of the widest marketing networks with more than 2000 branches and 65 area offices of LIC and also access to more than half a million agents in the country. It was promoted as Life Insurance Corporation on 19th June 1989 and a public issue was made in 1994. It provides house loans at an attractive rates of interest. LICHFL facilitates home loans to Resident Indian as well as Non-Resident Indian (NRI) along with providing various facilities to their esteemed customers like Green Channel, step-up EMI's as well as special facility to NRI's in the Gulf region. LICHFL, Resident Indians and NRI's can avail of home loans for several purposes, like purchase, construction, repairing and renovation or for purchasing a plot. Pensioners can also avail the benefits of LIC Home Loans. LIC Griha Prakash and Griha Laxmi loans are for purchase and construction of properties and the maximum loan offered can go up to Rs 1 crore. In both the cases, the housing finances upto a maximum of 85 per cent of the cost of the property which is inclusive of agreement value, stamp duty and registration charges. The maximum loan amount can be upto Rs.10 lakh and the loan to property cost does not exceed 85 per cent of Cost of Repairs or 25 per cent of Market Value of Property, whichever is lower. LIC Griha Prakash loans are meant for extension of residential units and the loan amounts range from Rs. 25,000 to Rs.1, 00, 00,000. In 2005, it provided major finance to individuals ranging upto 90 per cent and the remaining to others. The maximum repayment period can be upto 20 years or retirement age or 70 years of age, whichever is the earliest[18].

LIC Marketing Net work in India

- 6 regional offices and 115 area offices backed by a chain of camp offices in nationwide.
- 16 Back Offices spread across the country conduct the credit appraisal and administrative functions.
- One international office in Dubai

Performance of LICHFL

During the period under review, the company sanctioned Rs. 999 crores and disbursed Rs. 938 crores in the Individual

Loan category registering a growth of 14 per cent and 6 per cent respectively. Outstanding Mortgage Portfolio as on June 30, 2005 was Rs. 12889 crores as against Rs. 10222 crores as on June 30, 2004, showing a growth of 26 per cent. The company's total interest income for the quarter ending June 2005 was Rs. 271 crores as against Rs. 233 crores in the corresponding quarter last year registering a growth of 16 per cent. Interest expenses of the Company for the period were Rs.193 crores as compared to Rs. 160 crores in the quarter one last year. The company's total income for the quarter ending June 2005 was Rs. 286 crores as against Rs. 248 crores in the corresponding quarter of the previous year, constituting a growth of 15 per cent. Net profit of the company for quarter ended June 2005 was Rs. 50.18 crores as against Rs. 41.87 crores in the quarter ending June 2004, showing a growth of 20 per cent. The National Housing Bank (NHB) has revised the Non-Performing Assets (NPAs) recognition norms with effect from 31.3.2005. As per the new norms, a loan is classified as a NPAs if it is 90 days overdue, as against six months past due (earlier norms) in the previous year. LIC Housing Finance Director and Chief Executive, Mr. S. K. Mitter, said, "during the period under review, sanctions and disbursements showed an improved growth and this trend is expected to continue going forward. The income and net profits also registered healthy growth on account of a buoyant loan growth[19].

General Insurance Corporation

The General Insurance Corporation (GIC) started functioning from May 1971, and was nationalized in January 1973. It has four subsidiaries; The Oriental Fire and General Insurance Company, The United India Fire and General Insurance Company, The New India Fire and General Insurance Company and The National Insurance Company. The GIC started providing housing finance from 1977. As per the GIC guidelines, it gives loans to the State Governments for Social Housing Schemes to the extent of 20 per cent of its investable funds and 15 per cent to HUDCO. It also sanctions housing loans to its staff. Thus, around one-third of fresh accretions to its investable funds are to be invested in the housing sector[20].

Commercial Banks and Housing Finance

The commercial banks have been the largest mobilize of household savings in the country. But these banks did not enter the housing finance sector till the late sixties. The RBI being the apex body of commercial credit has been effecting changes from time to time to meet the household needs of the society. Housing, which was one of the sectors untouched by commercial banks till their nationalization, has now become an important segment of commercial credit provided by public as well as semi-public sector banks. Although during the initial years of nationalization, the role of commercial banks in providing housing finance was by and large absent. Execution of the social responsibility by earmarking a part of the overall credit lending was a reality during 1976[21]. Since 1970s, the scope of investment by commercial banks has been expanded to extend financial services for housing activities to individual households and to provide term loans at concessional rates of interest to the public housing agencies. This initiative was more appropriate from the viewpoint of the rich resource base of the commercial banks on the one hand and investment crunch in the housing sector on the other.

Introduction for Housing Finance

The role of commercial banks in providing housing finance to various income groups of house builders during the two and a half decades of their nationalization has been commandable. In fulfilling social obligations, there have been three important initiatives as far as housing finance is concerned. First, increasing the number of participatory institutions, i.e., commercial banks in India and outside the country the number of group of commercial banks has increased from three–State Bank of India (SBI) and its subsidiaries, nationalized banks (NBs) and other scheduled commercial banks (OSCBs) – during the 1970s to four with the entry of regional rural banks (RRBs) during the 1980s. Similarly, during the 1990s, foreign commercial banks (FCBs) were allowed into the domain of housing finance, in addition to the major Indian commercial banks. Inclusion of RRBs and FCBs was to respectively augment the supply of finance and ensure competitive environment for the Indian banks, and subsequently bring down the cost of housing credit gradually. To provide impetus to rural housing was the principal motive behind the inclusion of RRBs (NHB 1996). Earmarking of funds exclusively for housing activities and upward revision in the scale are a welcome step in the context of huge requirement of funds at competitive price to meet the financial needs of the non-poverty groups and have-nots. In the course of over 25 years of nationalization of commercial banks, the RBI has directed the banks to earmark funds exclusively for the purpose of financing housing and the scale has been revised twice so far.

Housing Finance and Incremental Deposits

Initially 0.5 per cent of the incremental deposits of the previous financial year were earmarked and all commercial banks were expected to finance housing on this basis for over one decade, from 1976 to 1989-90. From the financial year 1990-91, all scheduled commercial banks were advised to earmark housing finance up to 1.5 per cent of the incremental deposits. The revised scale was in operation for nine years till 1998-99. Then came the second upward revision during 1999-2000. Accordingly, commercial banks have now been advised to compute their share of minimum housing finance allocation at 3 per cent of their incremental deposits. However, banks were also given freedom to exceed the limit for housing allocations (RBI 1998-99). It is hardly necessary to point out that incremental credit ratio was to meet the changing needs of the time for the purposes[22].

Housing Credit Limit

There are three types of sub-targets within the housing credit limit.

- The first housing credit limit is the direct financing for individuals and groups of individuals. While extending direct financing for housing, Under the 20 Point Economic Programme, banks were advised to ensure that at least 50 per cent of the amount is further earmarked for scheduled castes and scheduled tribes (SCs and STs), economically weaker sections (EWS) and low-income groups (LIGs), and the remaining 50 per cent for rural and semi-urban areas (RBI 1991-92 and 1987-88).

- The second housing credit limit is the term loan to housing finance agencies like Housing and Urban Development Corporation (HUDCO) and State Housing Boards. In fact, these types of intermediary institutions are entitled to a concessional lending rate at 3 per cent below the rate of credit if 75 per cent of dwelling units are meant for EWS and LIGs.
- The third housing credit limit is the investment in the form of subscriptions to the guaranteed bonds and debentures of HUDCO and the National Housing Bank (NHB). Although commercial banks were expected to strictly adhere to the sub-targets up to the mid-1990s, sub-targets were, however, withdrawn in order to provide flexibility to banks in the deployment of housing allocations (RBI 1996-97).

Similarly, the restriction on the quantum of housing loan, which was up to Rs.3 lakhs per individual, was also withdrawn. Now, housing loan exceeding Rs.3 lakhs per individual is provided by banks at a little higher rate of interest, which is not necessarily a part of the housing finance allocation. Furthermore, to boost housing activities, other facilitating guidelines were issued (RBI 1998-89). Commercial banks can extend housing loans against LIC (Life Insurance Corporation) policies, promissory notes, shares and debentures as security if the mortgage of guarantee is not feasible. Providing composite loans for acquisition and development of land construction of housing units with infrastructure (water, drainage facilities, electricity and roads) for individuals as well as public agencies is also a part of the overall financing for housing by banks. After nationalization of commercial banks only the total credit under "*personal loans*" has been reported without bifurcating it for various activities including housing[23].

The RBI's Working Group on Housing (1978) under Chairmanship of R.C. Shah in its report on "Finance for Housing Schemes" estimated that the total annual advances of banking sector averaged at Rs.75 crores till 1980 and Rs.100 crores in 1981. Commercial banks do not lend money for more than 10 years for any housing scheme, because long-term housing loans have problems like (i) problems of liquidity arising out of the high statutory reserve ratio imposed by the RBI, (ii) lack of technical and financial expertise for appraising housing finance proposals and (iii) the feeling that housing is basically a speculative activity in nature. Another problem for banks is that of security, against which they have to lend for housing[24]. Commercial bank has issued at Rs.1 lakh to above Rs.8 lakhs the housing loans in 240 months for the construction purpose and any renovations are 120 months in the last six years i.e. 2000 to 2006. The interest is charged at 8 per cent to 13 per cent respectively. On recognizing the prospects in the housing sector more commercial banks are coming forward to establish specialist housing finance institutions. In addition to the above agencies the Central and State Governments, Unit Trust of India (UTI), provident fund, employers, and other housing finance companies have been extending financial assistance to augment the housing stock in the country by direct and indirect financing.

Criticism

Housing finance system, in general, and commercial banks, in particular, is not free from criticism. Rather, it is intriguing to note that the housing finance system is catering only to the needs of groups in urban areas that can afford housing and has left out the common person's financial needs. Rural financial needs for housing remain untouched. The position of commercial banks is not different from that of housing finance system, as far as housing finance is concerned, although the former has a huge network of institutions in rural areas. Commercial banks too were hesitant to finance housing (owing to its long-term nature) especially in rural areas during the first two decades of nationalization. In the wake of the above apprehensions fixing up of sub-targets within the earmarked credit for housing, which is the third initiative of the RBI, has provided an impetus to housing in rural areas and to some extent for economically weaker sections.

National Housing Bank (NHB)

National Housing Bank is the most important source of indirect finance in formal housing sector. The NHB that provides refinance to all the housing finance institutions finds itself a very respectable place in the housing finance sector. The Idea of forming an apex institution for housing finance in India has been evolved over a period of time. Right from 1971, on the recommendations of the study group appointed by the Banking Commission and the working group on housing finance, which was appointed by the Reserve Bank of India, felt that the housing problem was so acute that there was a need for a specialized system to address the needs of the housing sector. The working group recommended the establishment of a well-developed financing institution in the country exclusively to serving the housing sector. The working group's proposal to create a specialized institution for housing finance at the national level came to occupy centre stage in order to promote the utilization of public funds and to take up the task of promoting decentralized financial institutions which will serve all groups of people in the country. Based on the above recommendations a proposal to set up the National Housing Bank (NHB) was initiated by the Ministry of Urban Development[25].

The NHB was established on 9th July 1988. Under the National Housing Act 1987, to function as an apex bank, on the lines of the Industrial Development Bank (IDBI) and the National Bank of Agriculture and Rural Development (NABARD). The National Housing Bank Act envisages that NHB is the primary agency to promote housing finance agency at regional and local levels and to provide financial and other support to such agencies. The NHB (Amendment) Act, 2000. has vested the bank with wide power to regulate the Housing Finance Companies (HFIs). NHB has been striving towards the goal of 'Shelter for All'. The motto of NHB is 'Small Man First'[26].

The authorized and paid up capital of the bank at present is Rs.350 crores, wholly owned by the RBI. The Central Government is now authorized to increase the authorized capital upto Rs 2000 crores. Moreover, the central Government, schedule banks, public financial institutions can subscribe to the increase the share capital and other institutions approved by the central government besides the RBI [27].

Objectives of NHB

As an apex institution, the principal aim of NHB's involvement in primary lending institutions falling into various categories to serve as dedicated outlets of assistance to the housing sector. Specially, NHB has set for itself the following major objectives[28].

- to provide a sound , healthy , viable and cost effective housing finance system to cater to all segments of the population;
- to make housing more affordable;
- to establish a net work of housing finance outlets to adequately serve different regions and different income groups;
- to encourage public to emerge, primarily, as facilitation and suppliers of serviceable land;
- to encourage flow of credit and real resources to the 'small man first':
- to upgrade the housing stock in the country ; and
- to augment the supply of land and building material for housing;

Functions of NHB

The functions of NHB are specified below:

Promotion and Development: NHB is entrusted with the task of promotion and development of housing finance companies. It also conducts training programmes for the housing finance companies and financial assistance and faculty support to the National-Cooperative Housing Federation for organizing training programmes in the fields of housing co-operatives.

Regulation and Supervisions: As per the regulatory and supervisory authority in the field to housing finance, the NHB Act has vested NHB with the following powers

- Power to inspect
- Power to collect information
- To regulate or prohibit issue of prospects or advertisement soliciting deposits of money.
- To collect information from housing finance companies and to issue directions (Sec 31)

Financing: As an apex bank, the NHB provides both direct finance and indirect finance for the housing sector.

Programs and Schemes

Various programmes and schemes[29] have been implemented by NHB since 1990. Some of the important features of these programmes and schemes are listed below.

Home Loan Account Scheme (HLAS): The NHB formulated Home Loan Account Scheme (HLAS) in July 1989 with a few important features like,

- to encourage saving in advance of the decision to acquire a house;
- to provide housing loans at cheaper rates, particularly to the low income category.
- The outstanding amount of HLAS held in the books of the designated banks and housing finance companies as on March 31, 2002 was Rs.159.88 crores.

Capital Gains Bonds Scheme (CGBS): Under the Finance Act, 1989, NHB launched its Capital Gains Bonds Scheme (CGBS) on July 20th, 1990. This scheme is expected to enable NHB to mobilize funds at a comparatively lower cost, which can be utilized in providing the financial assistance to housing finance institutions at a lower rate of interest. The bank has mobilized

Rs.155 crores under this scheme. The features of these schemes are that wealth tax exemption, have a maturity period of three years, and carry 9 per cent interest per annum.

Land Development and Shelter Projects (LDSP): Under NHB guidelines, commercial banks and HFIs have a right to provide finance for projects like LDSP to public agencies such as Housing Boards, and Area Development Authorities (ADA), Co-operative Societies and Professional Developers.

Rural Housing scheme (RHS): NHB grants loans to public and private institution for Rural Housing Scheme provided the borrowing institution proposes the scheme.

Golden Jubilee Rural Housing Finance Scheme [GJRHFS]: In order to tackle the problems of growing needs and housing shortage in the rural areas of the country, the Union Finance Minster announced in his budget speech 1997-98, the formulation of the Golden Jubilee Rural Housing Finance Scheme (GJRHFS) by NHB 1997-98. The scheme is being implemented through scheduled public sector commercial Banks, State Co-operative Banks, RRBs, dedicated Housing finance companies and Apex Co-operative Housing Finance Societies (ACHFS) and also through the co-operative Agricultural and Rural Development Banks (ARDBs).

Training

- As a part of the training and developmental activities, NHB has been conducting training programmes for the personnel of HFCS/Public agencies apart from providing design and faculty support to banks/HFCs for conducting training programmes .
- NHB's endeavor has been to design and conduct training programmes for the personnel of primary lending agencies engaged in providing housing finance viz. HFC's, scheduled commercial banks, ARDBs, ACHFS, Development, Authorities, Housing Boards and the like.
- NHB has extended training assistance for implementing agencies and awareness building programmes to ensure effective implementation of the scheme.

Role of NHB in Housing Finance

The National Housing Bank continued its support and assistance in promoting a healthy housing finance sector in the country. The NHB completed its sixteenth year of functioning as the apex institution to promote the housing finance system and provide financial and other support to housing finance institutions in the country. The NHB has been undertaking measures for capacity building for the housing finance system and for improving the credit absorption capacity of the sector. The bank continued to expand its financial assistance to the housing sector by introducing innovative products and liberalized schemes in tune with market demand. The thrust for the development of the secondary mortgage market was renewed and the bank's efforts were continued to introduce mortgage credit guarantee in the country[30].

INFORMAL SECTOR

In our country, the informal sector has played a significant role in extending financial assistance for housing, especially to the poor and low-income households. The informal sector has been in a position to expand its activities because of the inaccessibility of the formal sector to the poor and the low-income group people. The informal sector has been quite successful despite several disadvantages because of the absence of cumbersome formalities.

Among informal sources the lion's share is accounted for by the households' personal savings. The other informal sources are the own money of households adjusted by disposing off their other physical assets like own savings and borrowings from relatives, friends and money lenders. The reference to provision of housing loans to employees and sale of houses on hire purchase basis is also worth mentioning under informal sector though it is not easy to judge the extent of contribution made by this group to the housing sector due to non- availability of accurate information[31].

Table 5
Interest Rates of Housing Finance Companies

Finance Company	*Loan Period*	*Less than 10,000*	*10,001 to 25,000*	*25,001 to 50,000*	*50,001 to 2 lakhs*	*2 lakhs to 5 lakhs*	*5 Lakhs to 10 lakhs*	*10 lakhs to 15 lakhs*	*15 lakhs to 25 lakhs*	*25 lakhs to 30 lakhs*	*30 lakhs to 50 lakhs*	*50 lakhs to 1 crore*
HDFC Ltd (Resident Indians) #	Upto10 yrs	12.50	13.50	13.50	13.50	13.50	13.50	14.50	14.50	14.50	14.50	-
HDFC Ltd (Resident Indians) #	10-15yrs	12.50	13.50	13.50	13.50	13.50	13.50	14.50	15.00	15.00	15.00	-
HDFC Ltd (Loans for NRI's) #	Upto 5 yrs	12.00	12.00	12.00	12.00	12.00	12.00	12.00	12.00	12.00	12.00	-
HDFC Ltd (Loans for NRI's) #	5-7 yrs	13.00	13.00	13.00	13.00	13.00	13.00	13.00	13.00	13.00	13.00	-
LICHousing #	Upto 5yrs	-	12.00	13.50	13.50	13.50	13.50	14.50	15.00	15.00	15.00	-
LIC Housing #	15-20yrs	-	12.50	14.00	14.00	14.00	14.00	15.50	15.50	15.50	15.50	-
GIC Housing	upto15yrs	-	13.50	13.50	13.50	13.50	14.00	15.00	15.00	15.00	-	-
GIC Housing	15-20yrs	-	13.75	13.75	13.75	13.75	14.25	15.25	15.25	15.25	-	-

Note:

\# These banks use Annnual Reducing Balance for calculations. All other Banks use Monthly Reducing Balance.

\## From 2 lakh to 3 lakhs interest rate is 13.50% & from 3 lakhs to 5lakhs interest rate is 14.00%

Source: Indiaatbest.com

INTEREST RATE STRUCTURE

Interest rates of housing finance companies are maintained in Table 5. HDFC, LICHF, NHB and other banks offer two types of interest rates, viz., fixed rate and adjustable/floating/flexible rates.

Under fixed rate of home loans, the rate of interest remains fixed for the entire loan period[32]. Under adjustable/floating rate, home loan, interest rate of is linked to Prime Lending Rate (PLR) and the rate fluctuates whenever there is change in PLR. In such a case, the (EMI) will not change. If interest rate goes up interest component in Equated Monthly Installment (EMI) will increase and the principal component will reduce, resulting in an extension of loan tenure and vice versa. The customers have a choice to choose either fixed rate of interest or flexible rate. Customers of HDFC, LICHF, NHB and other banks can change to floating rate form fixed rate, by paying conversion charges of 0.5 per cent of the principal amount outstanding.

REFERENCES

1. Ramesh Babu, G., Financial Services in India, New Delhi: concept building publishing company, 2006, p.4.
2. Anil Khandelwal, K., Housing finance increasing competition on, chairman, BOB Housing Finance Ltd, New Delhi: Charted Accounts, November 2001, p.18.
3. K.V.Varghese, K.V., Housing Problem in India, Pune: Gokhale Institute of politics and Economics, April 1995, p.267.
4. Housing finance sector will grow 24 pc in five yeas, Mumbai: Financial daily from Hindu, Wednesday, December 11th, 2002, p.7.
5. The Hindu, Friday, Bangalore (Edit), Bangalore: October 29th-2004 p.17.
6. Economic Times, Pune (Edit), Pune: Friday 24th February 2006, p.7.
7. Report on Trend and Progress of housing in India, New Delhi: National Housing Bank, 2005, p.15.
8. Ibid , p.25

9. www. NCHF.com.
10. www.planningcommission.com.
11. www.hudco.org.
12. HDFC, Bombay: Annual Reports, 2000-01, p.4.
13 The Hindu, Business Line, Andhra Pradesh: June 3, Saturday-2006, p.7.
14. www.HDFC.com
15. HDFC, Bombay: Annual Reports, 2005-2006, pp.16-21.
16. www.HDFC.com
17. www.HDFCbank.com
18. www.lichousingfinance.com
19. www.licofindia.com
20. www.gichousingfinance.com
21. Mahadeva, M and Thara Bai, Housing Finance : can Commercial Banks meet people's Housing Finance needs?, Bangalore: Social and Economic Change, Nagarabhavi, Vol.34, NO.1,Oct-Dec 2001. p.57.
22. Ibid, P.59.
23. Ibid, P.60.
24. www.reservebankofindia.com
25. www.nhb.org.in
26. Sudhakar Reddy, K., Commercial Banks and Housing Finance in India, UGC National Seminar, and Government College for Men, Puttur: Aug 16th -17th, 2006, p.3.
27. Financial Service in India (2006), op.cit., p.533
28. Ibid, p.534.
29. Ibid, p.537.
30. National Housing Bank, New Delhi: Annual Reports, 2000 to 2006.
31. Trend and Progress of Housing in India, New Delhi: National Housing Bank, 1992, p.52.
32. www.housingfinance.com

CHAPTER–3

DESIGN AND METHODOLOGY

INTRODUCTION

House is one of the basic necessities of human life. It is a basic need ensuring a modicum of decency and privacy. Housing and quality of living are intimately related. Good housing increases productivity of people. The life styles and culture of people are also reflected in the type of their dwelling units. The construction sector has a very close linkage with several other major sectors notably steel and cement. A general upsurge in construction activities not only increases the corpus of housing stock in the country, but also acts as a substantial fill-up to industrial and employment generating activities. Therefore, housing has been one of the areas of special focus in the recent policies of the government. With a booming economy and an enviable future ahead, India has become a promising country to live in. The banking sector has displayed continued vigor in the field of housing finance in the last few years and surpassed the minimum yearly housing finance allocation of 3 per cent of the incremental deposits as stipulated by the Reserve Bank of India by considerable margin.

STATEMENT OF THE PROBLEM

Housing has been recognized as one of the important indicators of standard of living. Housing offers financial security and social status. Finance plays a pivotal role in construction of houses though it is the desirous of every person having an own house. Investments in housing do not generate any substantial return to the investor and it remains as dead capital. Lending institutions also have to wait for longer duration to recover the amount lent to the borrowers of housing loans as against agricultural and industrial financing where the recovery of loans will be completed much earlier. Financial institutions constantly avoid involvement in provision of housing finance especially for the poor and middle class due to their lack of collateral security and steady income, involving high default risk and high transaction costs. So, housing finance in India is at nascent stage and the teething problems have to be sorted out to make investment in this sector more attractive. At this juncture, it is significant to assess the performance of housing finance system in India.

REVIEW OF LITERATURE

There are various studies made in the field of commercial banks in general and housing finance in India in particular. It is proposed to review the literature that exists in the field of housing finance by institutional agencies. Hence, an effort has been made to survey the relevant literature concerning housing finance.

Books

Bakshi Sinha and Arnold Heine Mann discussed housing and its role in the national economy. The study provides various housing and investment strategies in urban housing[1].

Sharma pointed out that there is a steep imbalance between demand and supply, which has shown a high peak in housing price, quite beyond the reach of those who are very much in the need of shelter[2].

Mathur described the housing problem in developing countries. The author also focused on the emerging housing needs and amelioration of housing condition[3].

Braja Bandhu Padhiari and Prakash Chandra Misra analysed the role of Housing and Urban Development Corporation (HUDCO) Ltd., in which an attempt has been made to evaluate the operational performance of HUDCO in rural housing sector in India with special reference to Orisa vis-a-vis other states[4].

Piyush Tiwari has given a clear picture of housing policies and programmes which require a careful estimation of household affordability and demand for housing. Besides, he pin-pointed the problem of multi collinearity [5].

Venkateswarlu emphasized the need for facilitating housing finance institutions to reach out the uncovered markets by rendering suitable financial services and improving the loan–absorbing capacity of the uncovered segments[6].

Vasant Desai concluded that the quantity and quality of housing could be increased by giving a small number of loans at higher ratios rather than a large number of loans at lower ratios. The author obviously lighted in ensuring proper deployment of credit within the housing sector from the bank's point of view[7].

Ramesh Babu described the different housing finance institutions and the schemes that provide finance to the needy housing individual groups[8].

Alpana Sivam and Sadasivam Karuppannan observed in their study that the housing demands, development of housing finance and formal housing agencies in both public and private sectors. According to them, they are neither fast enough to meet demand nor cheaply enough to reach the poor. As a consequence, an informal sector has emerged in almost all cities in India[9].

Huttman focused on the problems of housing in India. The study has enabled to highlight the emerging housing needs and the consequent suggestions to overcome the housing problems in our country[10].

Vinay Lal in his study has stressed the need for short-term and long-term resource mobilization policy. The short term strategy is to initiate the activities of the base level institutions and the long term strategy for aiming at large scale mobilization of savings of the household sector[11].

Kohli in his book revealed that housing finance system in the country represents a few players like Government and its

Housing Agencies. The present book raises many questions on the various aspects of housing finance related issues especially in financial aspects, operational aspects, and organizational aspects. The author has also tried to suggest possible solutions to related issues[12].

Kavita Datta and Gareth Jones in their book explored the linkages between formal and informal housing finance drawing upon the lessons of NGOs and micro-finance practices. Both public and private formal finance institutions have experienced great difficulty in lending below a middle-income client group, and are often reluctant to lend for the purpose of housing at all. The authors critically assess the impact of these schemes, and evaluate links between gender and housing finance[13].

Miglani examined the problems relating to demand for housing in planned and unplanned areas, housing investment among the salaried and non-salaried classes, investable surplus, rent structure, and the like. It also analysed the factors that determine the demand for home-ownership[14].

Articles

Singh and Sharma focused on the fact that the main objective of NHB, is to promote and establish housing finance institutions in the country as well as to provide refinance facilities to housing finance corporations and scheduled commercial banks. Their book also analyses the region wise disbursements of individual house loans, their portfolio amounts and defaults[15].

Chandramouli emphasized various aspects like the housing situation–quantity of housing and deficiencies, paucity of housing, need for public intervention and the like[16].

Boleat suggested that developing countries can learn from industrialized countries. However, it is clear that developing countries face more severe problems in respect of housing finance that are specific to them. The author briefly analyzed the types of housing finance institutions in order to put the position of developing countries in the context[17].

Bhattacharya revealed that the current scenario in the housing finance industry and SBI's strategies and the management's vision over the next few years[18].

Buraham Kelly analysed the problems of deficiency of houses, underdeveloped areas, underdeveloped countries, physical planning, housing activities, housing need, town sites, and housing problems [19].

Poyntz Tyler stressed the importance of slum clearance, blighted areas, urban renewal, redevelopers, finance agency, housing authority, the housing act and problems of families[20].

Gunnar Murdal observed that analyze the city ward migration which is under-utilized and in a false analogy with developed countries conceived of as progress in development[21].

Jasmindeep Kaur Brar and Pasricha have made an attempt to compare the housing finance provided by various institutions operating in different sectors and studied the problems that come in the way of financing the housing sector in the state of Punjab[22].

Rao stressed that the subject of housing finance should include not only the construction of house, but also the augmentation of infrastructural facilities[23].

Samantak Das stated that the National Housing Policy aims at mobilising resources and facilitating expansion of investment in housing. The author also highlighted the steps taken up by the Government to concentrate on upgrading and improving the facilities and creating a proper environment for housing finance activities by eliminating constraints[24].

Mahadeva concluded that scheduled commercial banks are largest institutional platform. They have to play a vital role in adopting new approaches and bring about customized and flexible mortgage products in active partnership with federal sources of state and local Governments, other Non-Profit Organisations and Formal Sector Institutions[25].

Aditya and Jaiswal opined that the country witnessed an unprecedented rise in land prices in the past ten years or so. They also concluded that investment in land is the best investment option[26].

Begum Anwara delineates the nature of housing as a social policy issue, where reinforced, co-ordinated planning and administration could ensure distributed benefits even to the poor[27].

Shri Krishna gave the present scenario of housing finance by the LIC. The article enabled to examine the performance of commercial banks and also to analyse the housing scenario in India[28].

Dholakia Bakul examined that the trends in housing stock in the Indian economy and analyzed the inter state differences influencing housing investment in India[29].

Shanti Tangri examined the some interrelations of urban growth, housing and economic development in India. The author also provided an estimation of the existing stock of housing, per capita living space, housing costs, likely growth of urban populations, housing needs, and investment requirements[30].

An article written by Mok Diana revealed the relationships of the desirability of home-ownership, price risks and the return on housing investment. The author argued that the price may undermine the desirability of ownership, using both a theoretical and an empirical approach. The empirical component uses current status data and a proportional hazard model to show the effect of risks and returns on households' risk rates to owners. The implication points to the inadequacy of the conventional housing finance arrangement, which provide little help for households to diversify or hedge the risk of home-ownership[31].

Rao's article depicted that the investment in economy by public and private sectors during the various plan periods. The author analysed the role played by public and private sector in housing finance activities in the country, since the beginning of the planning era[32].

Mahadeva and Thara Bai reviewed in their article the overall policy environment for commercial banks to earmark and provide direct housing finance to individual households and indirect term loans to public housing agencies. They also threw light on the sub-targets fixed to spread the benefits of housing allocations to the needy and neglected sections of the society and also suggested a policy options[33].

Khan stated that for millions of ordinary Indians, owning a home has remained a cherished dream over the decade. Today, a favorable mixture of various factors is helping them to realize that dream faster than ever before[34].

Pandit observed that the 'household' is the only surplus sector in the economy. The author suggested that by providing some kind of intermediation facilities the savings flow to the housing sector could be improved[35].

Renand Betrand has pointed out that weak existence of borrowed capital in the developing countries is the main cause for the inadequate development of housing. The author suggested that the problem of housing finance could be solved only through reconciling three differing objectives: improving competitions, increasing efficiency and stimulating long term finance[36].

Nasser Munjee stated that the mechanisms to link formal housing finance institutions such as HDFC to informal institutions working at micro level should be explored so that relevant institutions serve their constituents while at the same time being part of the net-work of specialized institutions[37].

Peer Smets outlined in his study self financing methods for construction that corresponds in their livelihood strategies of the urban poor and compared them with the supply side by focusing on different intervention schemes[38].

NEED FOR THE STUDY

In the decade between 1991-2001, India's urban population increased from 218 million to 285 million, a growth of 67 million. The projected scenario indicates a rising trend. The Planning Commission's Technical Group on Urban Perspectives and Policies has projected the urban population at 38.0 per cent for 2006-07. Further, the Planning Commission observed that the population of small and medium towns as a share of total urban population has been increasing rapidly. The liberalization of economy and industrial push are likely to encourage mass migration from villages to urban centres. In this connection, the urban policy has to be one that favours urbanization for the sake of development.

Having an own house is the minimum requirement whether it is in urban or rural area. Government is also launching programmes such as Indiramma Avas Yojana, Rajiv Swagruha for the poor and middle class people. But, these programmes are yet to reach the needy people. Households allocate more than 20 per cent of their income on housing. Low income group cannot afford to buy or construct houses at a time. The funds they can raise through incremental savings are no longer sufficient to develop a house within a meaningful time frame. For them, house loan is essential to have an own house. In this context, housing finance assumes much significance in the medium and small towns. But, it is observed from the review of literature that none of the studies have attempted to identify the problems of housing finance at micro level in small and medium towns which have much potential for housing activity and economic development. The present study is an endeavor to fill this gap.

OBJECTIVES OF THE STUDY

The following specific objectives have been set for the study:

- to appraise the housing situation in the country in general;
- to review the housing finance system in India ;
- to evaluate the performance of sample commercial banks in housing finance in the select urban area;
- to analyze the problems and experiences of customers availing housing loans ;
- to identify the problems of select commercial banks in the area of housing finance ; and
- to make relevant suggestions and recommendations towards effective and viable housing finance by commercial banks.

HYPOTHESES

The present study intends to formulate the following hypotheses to bring out certain conclusions concerning the performance of commercial banks in housing finance.

- There are no significant differences in the credit needs of individuals constructing residential houses.
- There are no significant differences in the select commercial banks in facing the problems regarding recovery of house loans.
- There are no significant differences in the awareness and satisfaction of the borrowers of housing loans from public sector commercial banks.

REFERENCE PERIOD

The present study needs a moderately lengthy period so as to arrive at meaningful and purposeful inferences. Therefore, the performance of the commercial banks in housing finance is evaluated over a 9 year period commencing from 1999-2000 to 2007-08. This period is significant as housing activity has been very active.

SAMPLE DESIGN

The study confines to Housing Finance by Commercial Banks in Kadapa Corporation. Presently, the banking structure in Kadapa Corporation comprises 19 Commercial Banks, i.e., 15 Public Sector Banks and 4 Private Sector Banks. The study has adopted Multi-stage sampling technique taking into consideration the banks, branches and loanees.

Stage I

Out of total 19 public sector commercial banks functioning in the Kadapa Corporation, 11 under public sector and all the 4 under private sector are not actively involved in housing finance activity. So they are excluded from the scope of the study. As such, the remaining four public sector commercial banks: State Bank of India (SBI) ; Syndicate Bank (SB); Andhra Bank (AB) and Indian Bank (IB) which are actively involved in housing finance activity have been selected for the study.

Stage II

The branch network of the sample banks in Kadapa Corporation is SBI-3;

AB – 3 ; SB – 3 and IB -1. From each of the select banks, one bank branch which is actively engaged in housing finance activity has been selected for an intensive study.

Stage III

The universe of the housing loan borrowers constitutes those individuals residing in the Kadapa Corporation who have availed loans from the four sample bank branches. The total housing loan borrowers are 1097 consisting 500 from SBI, 352 from AB, 179 from SB, and 66 from IB. Out of 1097 borrowers, 30 per cent borrowers are selected by applying the Random Sampling Technique. Thus, sample borrowers constitute 330 representing 150 from SBI, 106 from AB, 54 from SB, and 20 from IB.

The sample, therefore, finally constitutes 4 Public Sector commercial Banks, 4 bank branches and 330 sample housing finance borrowers.

DATA BASE

To achieve the set objectives, the study is based on both primary and secondary data. Primary Data is collected from the sample respondents who have taken housing loans from the sample bank branches. Pre- tested schedules were developed and administered for the purpose. The managers and staff members of select commercial banks are interviewed and discussions held in detail regarding various aspects of housing finance.

Secondary Data is obtained from the published reports by the Government of India, National Building Organization (NBO), RBI, Commercial banks. Data also have been collected from various reports published by the Five year plans of both Government of India and Government of Andhra Pradesh, National Housing Bank (NHB), Reports on Trend and Progress of Housing in India of NHB, Housing Development Finance Corporation (HDFC), the Housing Urban Development

Corporation (HUDCO), National Co-operative Housing Federation, LIC, GIC, Commercial bank and Reports on Trend and Progress of Housing in India. Besides, published and unpublished reports of various seminars and conferences held on the Housing Finance, Commercial Banks, and Housing in India were utilized.

Also various websites and journals like National News Review, Banking Finance, Yojana, Daily news papers like, the Hindu, Business Line, Business Standard, Economic Times, Financial Express, and local news papers are also referred to.

TOOLS OF ANALYSIS

The data collected from the primary and secondary sources have been analysed with the help of different analytical tools such as averages, trend analysis, comparative analysis, common size statements and percentages. Statistical tests are employed at appropriate contexts for arriving at meaningful inferences. Further, graphs and diagrams are also made use of to illustrate the facts and figures wherever necessary.

SCOPE OF THE STUDY

As mentioned earlier, the study confines to the performance of housing finance by selected commercial banks in Kadapa Corporation. The study, therefore, excludes other financing institutions, and also other categories of borrowers of housing loan like builders, professionals and beneficiaries under Government Schemes. The sample borrowers are the individual borrowers who have constructed residential houses only.

LIMITATIONS OF THE STUDY

Major limitations of the study are:

- Majority of the sample respondents belong to salaried class only.
- Secondary data have been collected from more than one source. Hence, there may be slight discrepancies between one source and another source on the same variable.

- A few respondents have been hesitant to disclose relevant information.
- In the case of annual income, few respondents are not able to give authentic information.

CHAPTER SCHEME

The study is presented in SEVEN Chapters.

Chapter 1 Housing scenario in India.

Chapter 2 Housing finance system in India.

Chapter 3 Design and Methodology.

Chapter 4 Performance of select commercial banks.

Chapter 5 Pattern of funds mobilized by the sample borrowers.

Chapter 6 Problems of borrowers and commercial banks.

Chapter 7 Summary of conclusion and suggestions.

REFERENCES

1. Bakshi, D., Sinha Housing Growth in India, New Delhi: Arnold Heine Mann, Published by India Pvt., 1976, pp. 1-3.
2. Sarma, Housing Finance in India, New Delhi: Sultan Chand Publication, 1990, pp. 22-25.
3. Mathur,G.C., Low Cost Housing in Developing Countries- New Delhi: Oxford and IBH publishing Co. Pvt. Ltd, 1977, pp. 22-25.
4. Braja Bandhu Padhiari and Prakash Chandra Mirsa, Rural Housing Finance, New Delhi: Discovery Publishing House, 2004 Vol-XV , pp. 218.
5. Piyush Tiwari., Housing Demand and Housing Policy in Urban India, Mumbai: Published by Urban Studies, November 1998, Vol 35, Issue 11, pp. 2111, 2129.
6. Venkateswarlu, U., Urbanization in India: Problems and Prospects, New Delhi: New Age International Private Limited, 1998, p.195.
7. Vasant Desai, The Indian Financial System, Mumbai: Himalaya publishing house, Fifth (edit), May 2002, pp. 575-595.
8. Ramesh Babu, Financial Service in India, New Delhi: Concept Publishing Company, 1987, p.245.

9. Alpana Sivam and Sadasivam, Housing and the Built Environment, Netherlands: Springer, Karuppannan, 1991, pp. 21-26.
10. Huttma, E.B., Housing in Asia: Problems and Perspectives, Jaipur: Rawat Publications, 1990, pp. 11-12.
11. Vinay, D. Lall, Housing Finance Scenario in Perspective of the National Housing Bank, New Delhi: Special Development Studies, 1987, pp. 1-6.
12. Kohli, V.K., Housing Finance Agencies in India , Assistant Director in the All India Council for Technical Education (AICTE), New Delhi: Mar 2007, (1st edit), Deep & Deep Publications Pvt. Ltd, pp. 15-25.
13. Kavita Datta; Gareth Jones, Housing Finance and Non-Governmental Organizations in Developing Countries, UK: Routledge, Volume 1, Part 2, December 1998, pp. 26–43.
14. Miglani, O.D., Urban Housing in Developing Economy, New Delhi: Government of India, Draft National Housing Policy, 1998, pp. 16-17.
15. Fulbag Singh and Reema Sharma, Housing Finance in India- A Case Study of LIC Housing Finance Limited, New Delhi: ICFAI Journal of Finance Economics, Vol IV, December 4, 2006, pp. 63-74.
16. Chandra Mouli, M., Housing in India- An Overview, New Delhi: Rehabilitation of Squatters in Delhi, August 1971, Vol.XVIII, No.5, pp. 5-10.
17. Boleat, M., Housing Finance Institutions, Lloyd Rodwin Boston: Allen Unwin, 1987, pp. 15-16.
18. Bhattacharya, T.S., Chief General Manager of SBI's personal banking division, Hyderabad: January 5th, 2002. pp. 1-2.
19. Buraham Kelly, Housing and Economic Development: The Report of a Conference Sponsored at, School of Architecture and Planning, University of Michigan, Michigan: Digitized, 15th August, 2006, p. 3.
20. Poyntz Tyler, City and Suburban Housing, New Delhi: H.W. Wilson Co, 2004, p. 5.
21. Gunnar Murdal, The Challenge of World Poverty, London: Allen Lane the Penguin Press, 1970, pp. 93-04.
22. Jasmindeep Kaur Brar and Pasricha, Housing Finance in Punjab:Sector-Wise Analysis, Punjab: Mata Gujri College, Fetengarh Sahib, pp. 46-54.

23. Rao, C.S., Financing Social Housing: A Review, Housing Finance in India, 1989, New Delhi: Himalaya Publications, pp. 152-159.

24. Samantak Das, Housing Finance - Some relevant issues, Finance and Markets, New Delhi: Management Accounts, December 1996, Vol. 31-Issue 12, pp. 888-893.

25. Mahadeva, M., Housing Finance Portfolio of Scheduled Commercial Banks (SCBs) - A Trend Analysis 2000-05, National Housing Bank, New Delhi: Occasational Paper 2007, pp. 6-9.

26. Aditya Jaiswal., Trends in the Housing Plan Market in India, Mumbai: Asian Economic Review, 1963, Vol 40, Issue-1, p.147.

27. Begum, Anwara, Urban Housing as an Issue of Redistribution through planning? The case of Dhak City, Dhak: Black Well Publishing, August 2007, Vol-41 , No-4 , pp. 410-418.

28. Shri Krishna, D., Housing Scenario in India-LICHFL, Urban India, Bangalore: 2002, Vol-7, Issue -2, p.2.

29. Dholakia Bakul, H., Macro Economic Analysis of Housing Demand and Housing Investment in India, New Delhi: Yojana, 2003, Vol 33, Issue-4, p.337.

30. Shanti, S., Tangri, Urban Growth Housing and Economic Development: The Case of India, Bangalore: Modernization in South Asia Studies July 1968, Vol-8, No-7, pp. 519-538.

31. *www.andf.co.uk*

32. Arimah, Ben, C., Housing Sector Performance in Global Perspective: A Cross - City Investigation, New Delhi: Published by Urban Studies, December 2000, Vol. 37, Issue 13, p. 2551.

33. Rao., D.V.R., Public Sector Investments as a Tool for Larger Private Sector Participation, Some design and planning considerations, Seminar on Economics of Housing in National Development, Ooty: 5-7 May, 1972, p. 5.

34. Khan,M.Y., Housing Finance: A Perfect Future, New Delhi: Chartered Financial Analyst, October 2002, p. 55.

35. Pandit, B.L., "Pattern of Household Savings and Asset Formation with Special Reference to Housing", Housing Finance in India, New Delhi: (1989) (Ed.) K.S.R.N. Sharma, pp. 110-122.

36. Renald Betrand, Housing Financial Institutions in Developing Countries", Washington DC: World Bank Staff Paper No. 658, World Bank, 1983, pp. 100-104.

37. Nasser M. Munjee, "Housing in the Economy-Some general perspectives and the Indian Case", Bangalore: Paper presented at World Conference on Housing, 1988, pp. 1-20.

38. Peer Smets, Housing Finance for the Urban Poor: An Analysis of Self-Help Practices from Hyderabad, India, Vrije University, New Delhi: Rawat, 2007, Vol XXIX, p.263.

CHAPTER–4

PERFORMANCE OF SELECT COMMERCIAL BANKS.

INTRODUCTION

The main aim of this Chapter is to present the profile and performance of select commercial banks in India. The importance of commercial banks in the progress of the economic development has been stressed from time to time by many economists and progressive bankers in the country. Commercial banks are the heart of the Indian financial structure with an ability to add to the supply and circulation of money by creating additional purchasing power in the country. The activities of the commercial banks in cooperation with the RBI have become dynamic, multi-directional and multi-dimensional in their growth as well. Commercial Banks are broadly classified according to their statutory functions and the area in which they function. In the last few years, the banking sector displayed great vigor in the field of housing finance and as stipulated by the Reserve Bank of India (RBI), the banks surpass the minimum yearly housing finance allocation of 3 per cent of an incremental deposit by a considerable margin. With a view to encouraging the growing contribution of the commercial banking sector in housing finance in the country, the Reserve Bank of India (RBI) issued certain measures for facilitating housing finance by the banks. The commercial properties are being assigned as a risk weightage of 100 per cent for capital adequacy purpose till the time of banks' loans and advances secured as mortgage on residential property. As a prelude to the study of financial performance of select commercial banks, the profile of these banks and the select branches are briefly presented.

PROFILE OF THE SELECT COMMERCIAL BANKS

As an introduction to the analysis of performance of Select Commercial Banks (SCBs), it is required to present a brief introduction of the select commercial banks. Four public sector commercial banks located in Kadapa Corporation have been selected for the purpose of this study. These are the State Bank of India (SBI), Andhra Bank (AB) Syndicate bank (SB), and Indian Bank (IB). These four commercial banks have been operating housing finance activities apart from their regular banking activities. However, analysis of their operations and problems are carried out in the succeeding Chapters.

Housing finance activity refers not only to the borrowers of housing loans but also to the lending banks i.e., Commercial Banks. The operational and financial health of the organization has to be ensured, if it is to survive and develop in the long run. The commercial banks are no exception to the principle. In this context, it is necessary that their lending has to be healthy not only in quantitative terms but also in qualitative terms. In this present Chapter, brief profile of the select banks and financial performance of the sample commercial banks presented.

State Bank of India (SBI)

State Bank of India (SBI) is India's largest commercial bank. The origin of State Bank of India dates back to 1806 when the Bank of Calcutta (later called the Bank of Bengal) was established. In 1921, the Bank of Bengal and two other Presidency banks (Bank of Madras and Bank of Bombay) were amalgamated to form the Imperial Bank of India. In 1955, the controlling interest in the Imperial Bank of India was acquired by the Reserve Bank of India. The State Bank of India (SBI) came into existence by an act of Parliament as successor to the

Imperial Bank of India. Today, State Bank of India (SBI) has spread its branches around the world and has a network of branches. SBI's International Banking Group delivers the full range of cross-border finance solutions through its four wings- the Domestic division, the Foreign offices division and the International services division[1]. SBI has a vast domestic network of over 14000 branches (approximately 14 per cent of all bank branches) and commands one-fifth of deposits and loans of all scheduled commercial banks in India. The Corporate Centre is in Mumbai and 14 Local Head Offices and 57 Zonal Offices are located at important cities spread throughout the country. The bank has total deposits of Rs.38004.60 crores and the advances of amounts to RS. 2618.01 crores in financial year 2007. The net profit is Rs.4407 crores during the same year. SBI of India has 52 foreign offices in 34 countries across the globe. The State Bank Group includes a network of eight banking subsidiaries and several non-banking subsidiaries offering merchant banking services, fund management, factoring services, primary dealership in government securities, credit cards and insurance. The eight banking subsidiaries are:

- State Bank of Bikaner and Jaipur (SBBJ)
- State Bank of Hyderabad (SBH)
- State Bank of India (SBI)
- State Bank of Indore (SBIR)
- State Bank of Mysore(SBM)
- State Bank of Patiala (SBP)
- State Bank of Saurashtra (SBS)
- State Bank of Travancore (SBT)

Technology Initiatives: There are certain technology initiatives in SBI:

- Fully computerized branches of the bank capture 76 per cent of the domestic business and 100 per cent of the forex business.
- Two innovative projects namely Electronic Nostro Account Reconciliation (ELENOR) and State Bank

Electronic Payment Systems (STEPS) were conceived, developed and successfully implemented with in-house expertise.

- Bank technology plan for enhancing customer service includes setting up 263 ATMs across the country. So far, bank has networked 100 ATMs across 8 major centres. With the addition of a few more cities and ATMs to the network, bank will have one of the largest ATM networks. Bank has already issued more than one million ATM cards to its customers.
- Other steps include Tele-banking at selected centres, electronic funds transfer at more than 500 branches for corporates etc. With all these initiatives, bank is thus moving closer to Anywhere, Anytime banking.
- Bank has constituted an Integrated Risk Management Committee, which will act as the apex committee for overall control of risk management functions. Bank is also developing MIS for better risk management and risk management models for different types of risks. Along with its technology initiatives, bank is well poised to meet the new challenges.

Select SBI Branch: It is one of the select bank branches of the present study. The main branch of SBI was established in the year 1923. Later it established its branches in Kadapa Corporation from 1992 onwards. There are six branches located in Kadapa Corporation for the year 2008. One bank branch which is actively engaged in housing finance activity has been selected for an intensive study. The specific select commercial bank branch is located in Yellarmukkapalli. It was established in the year 1992 in Kadapa Corporation. The bank branch has total accounts 15000 including housing finance. Bank technology plan for enhancing customer service includes setting up 3 ATMs across the Kadapa Corporation. It has one manager, two assistant managers and 50 members of staff[2]. Bank has not maintained Integrated Risk Management Committee in Kadapa Corporation.

Andhra Bank (AB)

Andhra Bank" was founded by the eminent freedom fighter and a multifaceted genius, Dr. Bhogaraju Pattabhi Sitaramayya. The Bank was registered on 20th November 1923 and commenced its activities from 28th November 1923 with a paid up capital of Rs 1.00 lakh and an authorized capital of Rs 10.00 lakhs. The Bank has crossed many milestones and the Bank's total business as on 30.09.2007 stood at Rs.71, 928 crores with a Clientele base of over 1.50 crores. The Bank renders services through 2013 Business Delivery Channels consisting of 1328 branches, 80 Extension Counters, 567 ATMs and 38 Satellite Offices spread over 21 States and 2 Union Territories as at the end of June, 2007. Besides, ATM sharing arrangements with several Banks include SBI group, IDBI Bank, UTI Bank, HDFC Bank, Indian Bank and others under National Financial Network Switch covering 19872 ATMs. Andhra bank provides state-of the-art services to its customers. All the branches of the bank are computerized and 850 branches are networked under core banking solution providing *'Anywhere Banking'*. The Bank also provides instant transfer fund facility through its branches. The bank has total deposits worth Rs.33922.41 crores and the advances worth of RS.22100.43 crores during 2006. The net profit is Rs.485.50 crores from the same year. The Bank has been ranked 5th in the 2005 Business Today Survey of India's Best Banks[3].

Technology Initiatives

The technology initiatives of the AB are:

- The bank opened its Representative Office in Dubai in May, 2006 and has received permission from Reserve Bank of India for opening Representative Offices at new Jersy.
- Bank has also launched "Smart Card" under Financial Inclusion at Gessukonda Warangal District (Andhra Pradesh) and it proposes to extend the same to other areas.
- Bank issued 27.26 lakhs of ATM/Debt Cards.

- Bank introduced low cost comprehensive health insurance scheme for all credit linked Groups under the name "Swashya Bima Yojana".

Select Andhra Bank Branch

The second select commercial bank branch is Main Branch of Andhra Bank which was established in Kadapa in 1951. It is one of the select bank branches of the study. There are three branches in Kadapa Corporation. Among three branches, select branch is actively engaged in housing finance activity in Kadapa Corporation. It has one Manager, 5 Asst. Managers and 13 staff members with 45000 customers, including housing finance loanees[4].

Syndicate Bank (SB)

Syndicate Bank was established in 1925 at Udupi, in Karnataka, by three visionaries-Sri Upendra Ananth Pai, a businessman, Sri Vaman Kudva, an engineer and Dr.T M A Pai, a physician-with the name "Canara Industrial and Banking Syndicate Ltd." The Bank was started with a capital of Rs 8000 and the objective behind starting the bank was primarily to mobilize small savings from the community so as to provide financial assistance to the local weavers who were crippled by a crisis in the handloom industry. In 1928, the Bank started the Pigmy Deposit Scheme under which it collected as low as 2 annas daily at the doorsteps of the depositors through its agents. The Pigmy Deposit Scheme is Syndicate Bank's Brand equity today and the Bank collects around Rs. 2 crore per day under the scheme. The name of the Bank was changed from "Canara Industrial and Banking Syndicate Ltd." to "Syndicate Bank Limited "in 1964 and the Head Office was shifted to Manipal. The Bank was nationalized in 1969. Today, the Bank has a branch net-work 1801 spread all over India. Syndicate Bank has won many awards over the years for its excellent performance[5].

Technology Initiatives

There are some technology initiatives in SB:

- All the 2100 branches are computerized/mechanised extending, accurate and prompt services.
- 7 day banking introduced in 209 branches
- Extended business hours introduced in 603 branches
- Demat facility introduced at Mumbai, Hyderabad, Bangalore, Delhi, Ernakulam and Vijayawada.
- 456 ATMs/ Cash Dispensers installed as on date Tele Banking facility introduced in 245 branches.
- 21st century will be dominated by Information Technology, knowledge and competition. Bank is gearing itself adequately to meet these challenges.
- Bank has planned to increase the coverage of Syndicate-Banking to 1500 branches as on 31st March 2007. This covers providing of e-Banking services through electronic channels viz. ATM, Telebanking and Internet banking.
- Knowledge and skill levels of employees are being upgraded on an on-going basis through strengthening of the training infrastructure with computer labs and other modern teaching methods.

Select Syndicate Bank Branch

The third select commercial bank branch is Syndicate Bank Main Branch. It was established in Kadapa before Independence on 1941. At present three branches are located in Kadapa Corporation. Three branches are computerized/mechanised extending, accurate and prompt services. The main branch is very actively engaged in the housing finance activity. It has one Manager, 8 Asst. Managers, 11 members of staff and the numbers of customers are 45000[6]. It may be observed that the branch was able to mobilize the deposits but lending was at low ebb in certain years.

Indian Bank (IB)

Indian Bank was established on August 15, 1907 as part of the Swadeshi movement. In 1969, the bank was nationalized along with 13 other banks. Indian Bank has an impressive international presence. The Bank has overseas branches in Singapore and Colombo including a Foreign Currency Banking Unit at Colombo. Indian Bank has 229 overseas correspondent banks in 69 countries. Indian Bank is engaged in diversified banking activities and has 3 subsidiary companies to look after them. These are: Indian Bank Merchant Banking Services Ltd, Indian Bank Housing Ltd and Indian Fund Management Ltd. Indian Bank are a front runner in specialized banking. The bank has 88 Forex Authorized branches inclusive of 3 Specialized Overseas Branches at Chennai, Bangalore and Mumbai exclusively for handling Forex transactions arising out of Export, Import Remittances and Non Resident Indian business. The bank has also 5 specialized NRI branches exclusively for servicing Non-Resident Indians and one Small Scale Industries Branch extending finance exclusively to SSI units. It has launched several innovative loan products like Artisan Card, Kisan Card, Kisan Bike Scheme, Yuva Kisan Vidya Nidhi Yojana to meet diverse credit needs of the farmers[7]. The total business of the bank crossed Rs.76000 crores as on 2006. The operating profit increased to Rs.1358.59 crores and net profit of banks are increased to Rs.1358.59 crores and Rs.3621.00 crores by the end of March 2006. Diversified banking activities are three subsidiary companies:

- Indian Bank Merchant Banking Services Ltd.
- Indian Bank Housing.
- Indian Bank Management Ltd.

Technology Initiatives

Technology initiatives of the IB are

- 100 per cent business computerization.
- 168 centres throughout the country covered under 'Anywhere Banking'.
- Core Service Banking (CBS) in 1520 branches and 77 extension counters/
- 596 connected Automated Teller Machines (ATM) in 220 cities/towns.

- Internet and Tele Banking services to all shared network.
- E-payment facility for corporate customers.
- Cash management services and Depository services

Select Indian Bank Branch

Another select commercial bank branch is Indian Bank (Main Branch). There is only one branch in Kadapa Corporation started in s1994. The total staffs working in the banks are one manager, five assistant managers and 6 other staff. It has a total accounts are 12000 including housing finance borrowers 8. It is obvious that net profit of the branch has gradually improved over period under reference. It may be said that all the three variables have depicted a rise.

Housing Finance Procedure by Commercial Banks

The select commercial banks sanction loans for construction/ purchase/extension/repairs of house flats/apartment and the like. Employees of the central and state governments, public enterprises and reputed private establishments, self-employed professionals and business people (with income tax assessment) and non resident Indians are eligible to take house loans from commercial banks. Companies and other corporate constructing houses can also seek loans from sample banks for their employees.

Sanction of loan amount is limited to 75 per cent of the cost of construction in case of rural/semi urban areas and 85 per cent in urban/metropolitan areas. About 40 per cent of gross monthly income is taken as repayment capacity of the borrower. Security for loans would be in the form of equitable mortgage by way of deposit of title deeds of house property. In addition to it, securities like LIC policies and National Saving Certificates equalent of 5 to 10 EMIs along with one/two guarantors are also insisted upon by select banks from its borrowers.

Loans are normally disbursed in two or more than three installments. Repayment of loans is generally allowed in equated monthly installments (EMIs) ranging between 5 and 20 yeas. The margin of loan is a minimum 15 per cent on project cost (cost of construction + cost of land). If land is already owned (either self-earned/inherited/acquired by way of gift) and loan is applied for construction purpose, cost of land (at market value certified by our approved Engineer) and construction cost together will be treated as project cost and land value can be considered for margin purpose and 15 per cent margin on project cost will have to be ensured. One per cent as administrative fee is collected from the borrowers[9].

FINANCIAL PERFORMANCE OF SELECT COMMERCIAL BANKS

The financial performance of select public sector commercial banks is carried out as the extent of housing finance depends on their financial strength. Financial performance refers the financial strengths and weakness to an enterprise. In fact, financial analysis is the process of making an analytical study of the financial and operational data contained in the profit and loss account and the balance sheet of a given concern and thereby satisfying the information needs of the internal and external users of such data.

The financial performance is the result of the continuous flow of the accounting cycle which starts with classification, recording, summarizing, presentation and analysis of data and ends with interpretations of the results obtained from such analysis[10]. The analysis and interpretation of the financial statements results in the presentation of information that will aid in decision-making by business managers, investors, creditors as well as other groups who are interested in the financial status and operating results of a business[11]. The financial performance of select commercial banks is evaluated mainly from three facets as specified:

- Liquidity performance
- Solvency performance
- Profitability performance

The relevant ratios are computed to make effective judgments about the financial performance of select commercial banks.

Liquidity Performance

Liquidity has been defined as the capacity to meet short term financial commitments, i.e., short term solvency. Sinkey defines "bank liquidity management as the process of generating funds to meet contractual or relationship obligations at reasonable prices at all times"[12]. In general, the contractual obligations of a banker are to meet deposits with drawals and/or borrowing repayments, and relationship obligations cover loan demand. However liquidity under contractual obligations is more important for the outside parties, i.e., depositors and lenders. One of the important measures of liquidity for the business enterprise is current ratio which is obtained by dividing current assets by current liabilities of a firm and is widely acceptable for measuring the business firm's short-term solvency, i.e., its ability to meet short term obligations.

Current Ratio

As a measure of short term/current financial liquidity, the current ratio indicates the rupees of current assets available for each rupee indicates the rupees of current assets available for each rupee of current liability/obligation. Current assets represents the cash and balance with RBI, balances with bank and money at call and short notice and other assets that get converted into liquidity cash within the short time. Current liabilities are the short term deposits, borrowings, bills payable other liabilities. The higher the current ratio is, the more is firm's ability to meet current obligations. It is also an indicator of margin of safety to the creditors of the firm. It is therefore necessary that the size of the current assets should be sufficiently larger than the current liabilities, so that the firm is able to pay its current maturing debts as and when due. Thus the current ratio measures the size of short term liquidity "buffer". Although there is no hard and fast rule, conventionally a current ratio of 2:1 (current assets twice current liabilities) is considered satisfactory. Current assets represents the cash and balance with RBI, balances with bank and money at call and short notice, investment, advances and other assets that get converted into liquidity cash within the short time. Current liabilities are the deposits, borrowings and other liabilities.

Thus, the current ratio is used not only as an indicator of the concern's ability to pay its current obligations but also to find out its capacity to carry on its operations efficiently. In the form of equation, the current ratio can be put as follows:

$$\text{Current Ratio} = \frac{\text{Cash and balance with RBI, balance with bank and money at call and short notice, investment, advances and other assets,}}{\text{Total current liabilities}}$$

Table 5
Current Ratio of the Select Commercial Banks

(in times)

Years	*SBI*	*AB*	*SB*	*IB*
1999-2K	1.04	1.03	1.03	1.12
2000-01	1. 04	1.03	1.04	1.10
2001-02	1.04	1.04	1.04	1.15
2002-03	1.04	1.04	1.04	1.18
2003-04	1.05	1.05	1.03	1.15
2004-05	1.05	1.05	1.04	1.14
2005-06	1.05	1.07	1.04	1.04
2006-07	1.20	1.08	1.04	1.08
2007-08	1.22	1.09	1.04	1.11
Average	1.08	0.93	0.70	1.12

Source: Compiled from the annual reports of the select commercial banks

Table 5 indicates the current ratio of the select commercial banks. It is observed that the average current ratio of IB is 1.12 times which is the highest followed by SBI, AB and SB with 1.08 times,0.93 and 0.70. It is evident that the current ratio of these banks hovoured a round 1:1. In other wards, the ratio has never touched the standard norm of 2:1 in any one of the sample commercial public sector banks. It may be inferred that the liquidity position of these banks far from satisfactory. Chart 1 represents the current ratio of the select commercial banks.

Chart 1: Current Ratio of the Select Commercial Banks

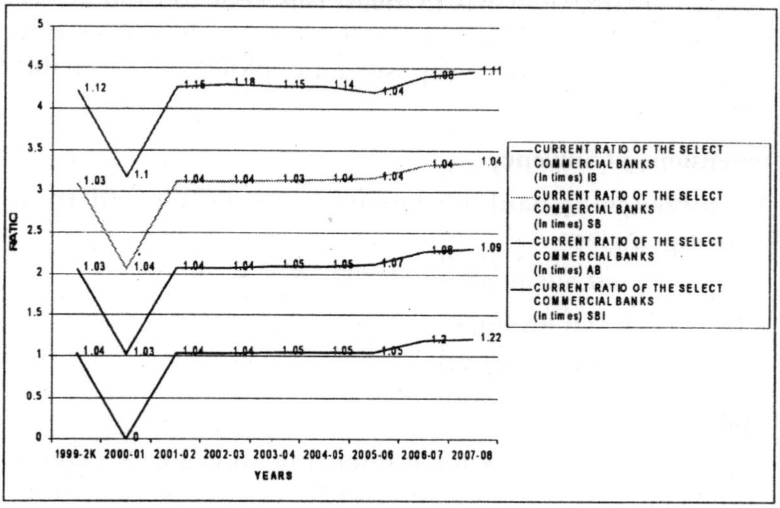

Long Term Solvency Performance

Solvency means ability to remain in business, i.e., not to be bankrupt. It is measured by a firm's ability to meet its present and future long term financial obligations in full, i.e., to have continued credit worthiness. As the last claim in a business is on shareholder's funds, it is necessary for the firm to have a sound capital structure relative to its operations. Solvency of the business firm is, therefore, a major consideration for lenders and shareholders alike as it ensures that the firm's operations are able to serve the long-term debt with payment of interest and principal installment and capital with dividend or appreciation. In the banking industry, solvency is interpreted in terms of an on-going /viable bank. Non-solvency in the banking industry occurs in many forms such as failure, moratorium, closure or merger. It is characterized by the same main factors-strong capital base and a sound capital structure, i.e., the composition of long term obligations.

The banking industry is a highly levered industry and its capital structure is characterized by a low equity base in relation to total assets. A bank requires very small amount of capital to create a large portfolio of deposits and loans as, being a service organization, has to invest very little in fixed assets. The essence of banking business is trust which enables it to mobilize large amount of deposits for deploying in profitable operations.

Dimensions of Solvency

The solvency of banking business can be viewed from following angles:

- Capital adequacy
- Financial leverage
- Adequacy of profit

Capital Adequacy

The most important factor influencing solvency is capital. Capital and all reserves and surplus available to equity shareholders. It is the last line of defence to meet the financial commitments of residual claimants in case a bank fails, closes or goes insolvent. Capital is the cushion between bank's unrealized assets and pending liabilities. It is basically a guarantee fund whose presence serves only maintenance purpose but absence or inadequacy is perilous. It is necessary for a bank not only to have its capital intact but also to ensure its adequacy corresponding tc volume of business.

The common item, the bank capital is related to total deposits and a minimum ratio of 10 per cent of deposits is considered safe for carrying on banking operations. The rationale behind using deposits as a base is that banks operating on this relationship of capital funds to deposits could be sufficiently profitable to attract the necessary capital through the sale of capital stock[13]. Thus, it may be said that capital in reality has no relationship with the amount of deposits. In terms of assets, the capital is first related to total assets of the bank and a percentage of total assets are prescribed for the capital adequacy.

Shareholders Fund to Risk Assets

The shareholders fund to risk assets ratio, wherein only risk assets were considered for determining the capital size. This measure has been more scientific and logical than all the other measures. The term risk assets represent total assets minus current assets and investments. Shareholders fund refers to one's own funds inclusive of capital, reserves and surplus. The basic aim of calculating the shareholders fund to risk assets ratio is to measure the relative interest of owners and creditors in the firm. From the creditors point of view, it measures the extent to which their interest is covered by owned funds. A very high ratio indicates better protection for the depositors and lenders of the bank. The ratio can expressed as mentioned below:

Shareholders Fund to Risk Assets = Shareholders Fund/ Risk Assets

Table 6
Shareholders Fund to Risk Assets Ratio of the Select Commercial Banks

(in times)

Years	*SBI*	*AB*	*SB*	*IB*
1999-2K	0.12	0.10	0.09	0.34
2000-01	0.12	0.10	0.09	0.29
2001-02	0.12	0.09	0.09	0.37
2002-03	0.12	0.10	0.10	0.04
2003-04	0.13	0.11	0.09	0.38
2004-05	0.11	0.10	0.08	0.32
2005-06	0.10	0.13	0.77	0.11
2006-07	0.11	0.14	0.75	0.21
2007-08	0.11	0.15	0.78	0.23
Average	0.12	0.11	0.32	0.25

Source: Compiled from the annual reports of the select commercial banks

Shareholders fund to risk assets ratios of the select commercial banks are portrayed Table 6. It is evident that the average ratio of shareholders fund to risk assets had varied between 0.11times in AB and 0.32 in SB during the period under reference. It may be observed that the ratio has not fitness any improvement among all the select commercial banks over the study period. The highest ratio was recorded in 0.78 times in SB in 2007-08 and the lowest being 0.04 times in IB during the year 2002-03. It is clear that shareholders equity is in sufficient in comparison to risk assets has the ratio had never exceeded one. Hence, it may be concluded that the depositors and lenders of the select commercial banks were not protected. In other words, these banks have not been performing better on the capital adequacy front.

Chart 2 shows the shareholders fund to risk assets ratio of the select commercial banks.

Chart 2: Shareholders Fund to Risk Assets Ratio of the Select Commercial Banks

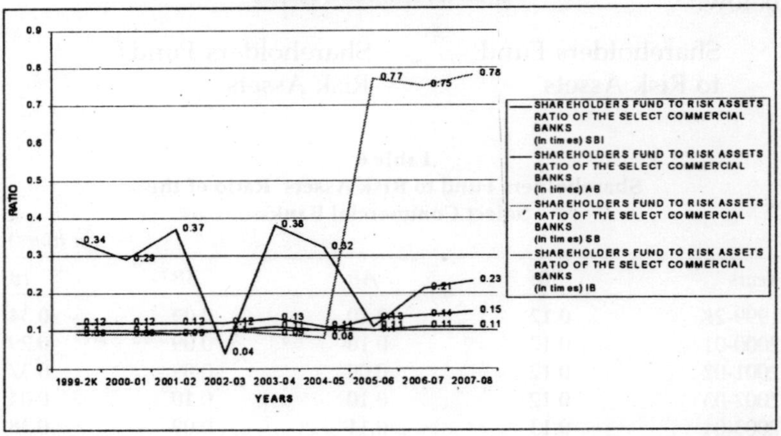

Financial Leverage

The other accompanying concept of capital is the financial leverage. Financial leverage is the business risk which a bank bears by trading on equity. Business risk is the larger risk which means expansion of business in comparison to quantum of capital. Both business risk and solvency risk are positively correlated. A bank having higher financial leverage, i.e., business risk will require more capital to reduce risk of probable failure. The relationship between financial leverage and risk exposure in a bank can be expressed by equity multiplier (EM) as follows.

Equity Multiplier = Total Assets/Total Equity Capital

Equity multiplier which measures the amount of assets pyramided on a bank's equity based is simply the reciprocal of the ratio of total equity capital to total assets. A higher equity multiplier means low capital base and vice versa. Generally, the banks by nature have a high degree of financial leverage, i.e., low capital and high assets. As the ratio is reciprocal of capital adequacy ratio, a very large equity multiplier indicates inadequate capital. In a risk-return framework, financial leverage increases a bank's potential risk as well as returns.

Table 7
Equity Multiplier Ratio of the Select Commercial Banks

(in times)

Years	*SBI*	*AB*	*SB*	*IB*
1999-2K	43.18	45.42	57.55	9.40
2000-01	52.34	45.31	58.84	10.64
2001-02	58.01	46.53	67.28	8.03
2002-03	63.25	61.70	72.96	7.73
2003-04	67.98	67.52	100.05	8.56
2004-05	78.85	81.82	110.40	9.59
2005-06	85.29	83.85	117.01	63.57
2006-07	107.65	98.02	119.21	67.67
2007-08	114.26	116.68	120.01	84.97
Average	74.53	71.68	91.26	30.02

Source: Compiled from the annual reports of the select commercial banks

Table 7 shows the ratio of total equity capital to total assets. The highest average ratio of 91.26 times is observed with SB and lowest average ratio with 30.02 times in IB. Total equity capital to total assets ratio has increased in all select commercial banks over the study period with the exception of SBI. But, in case of IB, an abnormal increment is observed in the year 2005-06 as the capital in the year has decreased abnormally. Thus, the equity multiplier of the select banks signifies acquisition of more assets relative to capital base thereby helping to improve the profitability of the banks.

Chart 3 depicts the equity multiplier ratio of the select commercial banks.

Chart 3: Equity Multiplier Ratio of the Select Commercial Banks

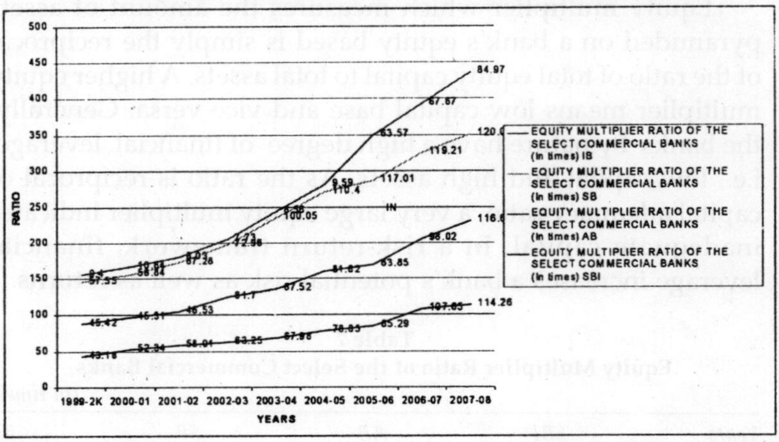

Adequacy of Profits

Regular and adequate generation of profit indicates operational efficiency of banking operations and ensures long term sustainability of bank. Profits are therefore, must for survival. A bank which is incurring losses or even has fluctuating profits shall not be able to keep its capital. A profit serve both borrowings and capital and is also a source of internal accruals for strengthening the capital base. However, before profits as retained earnings become part of capital, they are required to serve the borrowings with interests and rewarding the equity shareholders with dividends. If a bank defaults in servicing the borrowings, i.e., regular payment of interest as prescribed, it is not considered solvent. Though payment of dividends to equity shareholders is not mandatory, non-payment of dividend rate in a year are reflective of inadequacy of profit and thus, are not a positive sign of financial well-being. Profits are, therefore, important for both lenders and shareholders of a bank. The service aspects of net profit are given by following ratio.

Interest Coverage Ratio

Interest coverage ratio shows the number of times the interest charges are covered by the Earnings before Interest and Taxes

(EBIT), out of which they will be paid. In other words, it indicates the extent to which the earnings may fall without causing any embarrassment to the firm regarding the payment of fixed interest charges. Interest coverage ratio is calculated by dividing the operating profits or EBIT by the fixed interest charges on loans, thus,

Interest Coverage Ratio = EBIT/Interest Charges

A high coverage ratio is indicative of increased financial strength, i.e., solvency of a bank and vice-versa.

Interest coverage ratio of all select commercial banks is depicted in Table 8.

Table 8
Interest Coverage Ratio of the Select Commerical Banks

(in times)

Years	*SBI*	*AB*	*SB*	*IB*
1999-2K	1.24	1.28	1.17	1.26
2000-01	1.22	1.18	1.17	1.21
2001-02	1.29	1.29	1.20	1.17
2002-03	1.37	1.52	1.37	1.35
2003-04	1.50	1.71	1.64	1.52
2004-05	1.59	1.82	1.49	1.61
2005-06	1.55	1.51	1.48	1.48
2006-07	1.45	1.53	1.36	1.58
2007-08	1.42	1.37	1.25	1.14
Average	1.40	1.47	1.35	1.37

Source: Compiled from the annual reports of the select commercial banks

It is evident that interest coverage ratio on an average range between the lowest of 1.35 times and the highest of 1.47 times in SB and AB respectively. Though the ratio has witnessed more than one in other select public sector commercial banks. Solvency of these banks is not at the desired levels. The reason is, the EBIT levels are very meager to cover interest charges. On the whole, it may be said that the financial solvency of these banks is not satisfactory as the ratio had never touched the usual norm of 4:1. Interest coverage ratio of the select commercial banks is represented in Chart 4.

Chart 4: Interest Coverage Ratio of the Select Commercial Banks

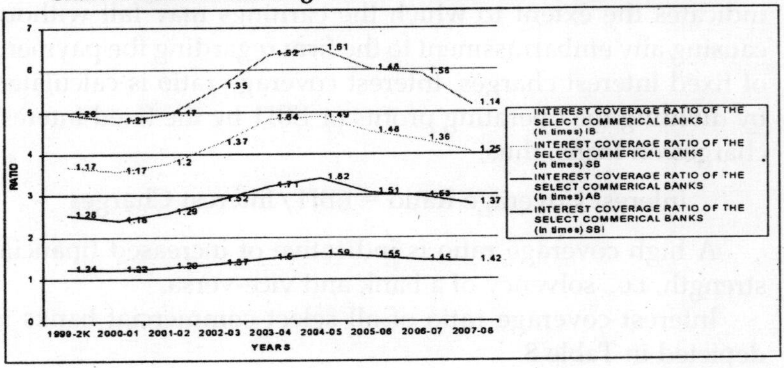

Profitability Performance

Profitability has been defined as ability to earn profit. It is measured in relative terms of either size, past year or peerage. The most commonly used measure of profitability is in terms of size, i.e., profit or loss divided by total assets. Sometimes profitability is measured by taking profit of two years to judge the more profitable year. Profitability has been an important criterion to evaluate the overall efficiency of a firm's operations. Being a relative measure, it is devoid of the pitfalls associated with interpretation of term profit. The concept of profitability is used and interpreted the same way both in a business firm and a banking company. Profitability in banking parlance denotes the efficiency with which a bank deploys its total resources to optimize its profits and thus serves an index of asset utilization and managerial effectiveness.

The relationship of profitability with other macro dimensions of solvency and liquidity has been that of risk return trade-off. The more risk a bank is willing to take in terms of less solvency and/or low liquidity, the more return it is able to earn. In other words, there is a direct inverse relationship between profitability and solvency/liquidity. An increased level of solvency means low leverage, low risk and consequently low profitability. In the same way high liquidity either increases interest burden or decreases earning ability, reduces risk and profitability becomes low.

Net Profit Ratio

Net profit to sales, otherwise known as profit margin is indicative of the position of sales that is left to the proprietors, after all costs, charges and expenses have been deducted. It differs from net operating profit, in as much as it is computed after adding non-operating income like interest or dividends on investments and deducting non-operating expenses such as loss on sale of old assets and provision for legal charges. The net profit margin is indicative of management ability to operate the business with sufficient success not only to recover from revenues of the period, the cost of merchandise or services, the expenses of operating the business (including depreciation) and the cost of borrowed funds, but also to leave a margin of reasonable compensation to owners for providing their capital at risk[14]. A high net profit margin would ensure adequate return to the owners as well as enable a firm to withstand adverse business conditions. The net profit margin i.e., net profit to sales, therefore, is widely used as a measure of a firm's overall profitability and is very useful to proprietors. The details pertaining to net profit margin in select commercial banks are embodied in Table 9 (Chart 5).

Table 9
Net Profit Margin Ratio of the Select Commercal Banks

(in percentage)

Years	*SBI*	*AB*	*SB*	*IB*
1999-2K	5.88	7.21	7.84	-24.44
2000-01	5.34	5.83	7.64	-12.75
2001-02		8.67	7.93	1.19
2002-03	8.43	14.40	10.21	6.18
2003-04	9.67	15.95	11.24	11.88
2004-05	10.89	19.62	9.27	11.88
2005-06	10.15	17.91	11.56	13.45
2006-07	10.10	17.51	11.32	13.72
2007-08	10.09	17.21	11.22	13.95
Average	8.63	13.81	9.80	1.30

Source: Compiled from the annual reports of the select commercial banks

The average net profit margin in the select banks have been varying between 13.81 per cent in AB and 1.30per cent in IB,

Chart 6: Net Profit Margin Ratio of the Select Commercial Banks

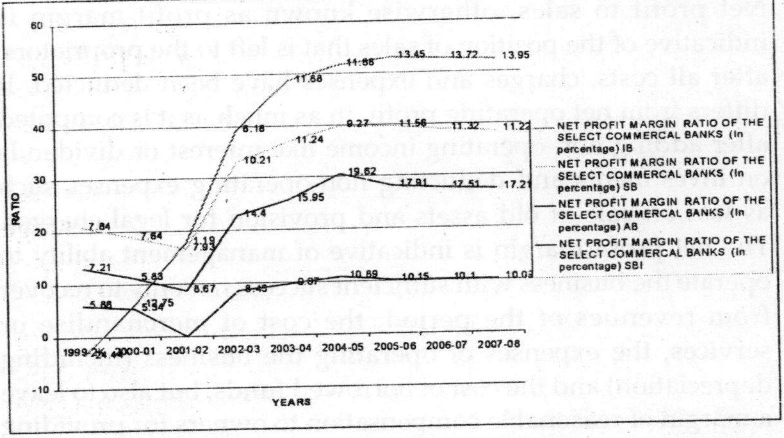

during the period of analysis. It is noticed that the net profit margin ratio in SBI has varied from 5.34 per cent to 10.89 per cent over the study period. In case of AB, the ratios have increased from 7.21 per cent in 1999-2K to 19.62 per cent in the 2004-05 and declined to 17.21 per cent in 2007-08. In case of SB, the ratios varied from the lowest 7.64 per cent and the highest of 11.56 during the study period. It is noticed that the average net profit margin of IB is very low due to presence of high rate of interest charges and the burden of heavy taxation.

In the IB, the net profit margin in the two yeas i.e., from 1999-2K to 2000-01 is negative with (-24.44) per cent and (-12.75) per cent. It may be concluded that of the overall net profit margin, AB is comparatively better than that of the remaining three sample banks.

Operating Ratio

The operating ratio signifies the relation between operating expenses and operating revenues. In the words of Kennedy and McMuller, "the term 'operating ratio' refers to the ratio of all operating expenses-cost of merchandise sold, selling expenses and general administrative expenses to net operating revenue[33]. It is considered an index of operational efficiency[15].

In the present context, operating expenses includes interest and other operating charges, establishment expenses and depreciation. And operating revenue includes interest earned, fees and other charges. Operating ratio is determined by diving operating expenses by operating revenues multiplied by 100.Higher the operating ratio lesser will be operating income (PBIT) and vice versa.

Table 10
Operating Ratio of the Select Commercial Banks

(in percentage)

Years	*SBI*	*AB*	*SB*	*IB*
1999-2K	26.50	21.46	30.98	36.12
2000-01	27.64	21.97	35.04	34.86
2001-02	21.22	19.45	32.55	25.97
2002-03	21.57	21.51	32.23	24.70
2003-04	24.28	22.65	29.81	31.11
2004-05	25.47	27.31	29.07	26.58
2005-06	27.01	27.39	30.93	28.29
2006-07	26.87	24.81	20.81	24.81
2007-08	21.87	19.37	16.99	22.76
Average	24.71	22.94	28.71	28.36

Source: Compiled from the annual reports of the select commercial banks

As seen from the Table 10 SB has the highest average operating ratio with 28.71 per cent followed by IB with 28.36 per cent, SBI with 24.71 per cent and AB with 22.94 per cent. It is evident that the operating ratio of fluctuated among the select commercial banks over the study period. The operating ratio depicted a decline in IB from 36.12 per cent in 1999-2K to 22.76 per cent in 2007-08. It indicate that this bank could control its operating expenses when compared to other select commercial banks. In other two banks the ratios has remained statistic with marginal fluctuations. Thus, can be concluded that the performance of IB is much better comparatively with regard to operating efficiency. Chart 6 shows the operating ratio of the select commercial banks.

Chart 6: Operating Ratio of the Select Commercial Banks

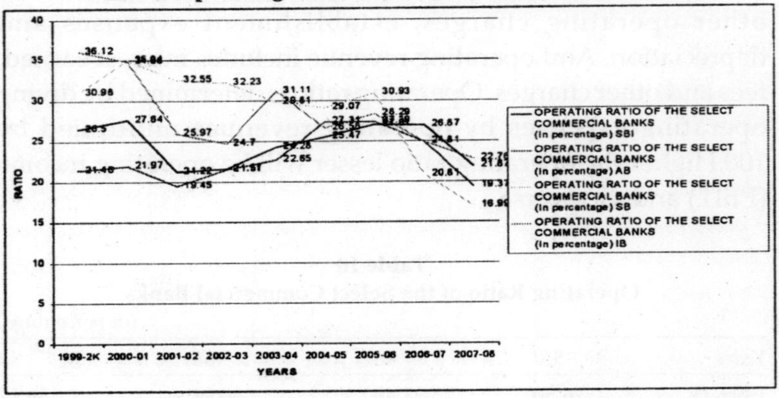

Return on Capital Employed

The most commonly used measure of profitability is to relate the profit output with the capital input and thus compute the rate of return on capital employed. The return on capital employed (ROC) indicates how well management had used the funds supplied by creditors and owners. Apart from this, it shows the earning power of the operating assets. The higher the ROC, the more efficient is the firm, in using funds entrusted to it. In other words, ROC is the key indicator of overall profitability of a bank. This can be calculated as follows:

$$\text{Return on capital employed} = \frac{\text{Profit before interest and tax}}{\text{Average net capital employed} \times 100}$$

The ROC is equal to the profit margin on sales multiplied by the capital turnover. The ROC is the result of the multiplication of the above two various-profit margin and capital turnover which by themselves are the products of a series of variables denoting various phases of business operations carried on during a given accounting period. Frequency of the turnover of capital invested and profit margin are the two factors on which profitability of capital invested depends. The overall profitability will improve if capital turnover or profit margin or both increase. The overall profitability will also increase, if the profit margin increases without any change or an improvement in the turnover ratio. The overall profitability can fail inspite of the increased capital turnover (or profit margin) if the profit margin (or capital turnover) has fallen at a greater rate[16]. A comparison of the ratio of ROC of a firm with the individual position of similar organisations over a period of time would provide sufficient insight into how efficiently the funds of owners and creditors are used.

Table 11 (Chart 7) depicts the return on capital employed of the select banks.

Table 11
Return on Capital Employed Ratio of the Select Commercial Banks

(in percentage)

Years	*SBI*	*AB*	*SB*	*IB*
1999-2K	8.34	8.32	6.97	8.14
2000-01	7.89	7.96	7.07	7.31
2001-02	8.77	8.98	6.71	6.84
2002-03	8.67	8.90	6.62	6.51
2003-04	7.06	8.32	5.74	6.01
2004-05	7.02	6.74	5.92	5.76
2005-06	6.41	5.59	5.25	5.78
2006-07	5.68	6.12	5.22	6.76
2007-08	5.86	6.95	5.19	6.81
Average	7.30	7.54	6.08	6.56

Source: Compiled from the annual reports of the select commercial banks

Chart 7: Return on Capital Employed Ratio of the Select Commercial Banks

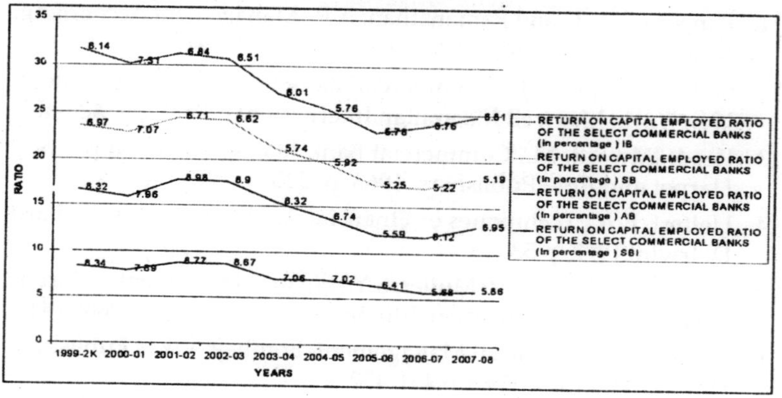

On the total average it is analyzed that the highest of 7.54per cent is recorded as return on capital employed in AB, followed by SBI with 7.30per cent, IB with 6.56 per cent and the lowest average is recorded in SB with 6.08 per cent. In analysis, four of these sample banks are registered as a remarkable rise in the ROC. It is pertinent to note that the rise in the ROC was primarily due to increase in profit margin and higher capital turnover in sample banks.

On the whole, AB and SBI have enjoyed reasonable return on their respective capital employed throughout the period of study.

REFERENCES

1. *www.statebankofindia.co.in*
2. Records of State Bank of India, Kadapa: 2004, pp.10-11.
3. *www.andhrabank.com*
4. Records of Andhra Bank , Kadapa: 2000, pp.7-9.
5. *www.syndicatebank.co.in*
6. Records of Syndicate Bank, Kadapa: 2002, pp.5-7.
7. *www.indianbank.ocm*
8. Records of Indian Bank, Kadapa: 2005, pp.4-6.
9. Choyal, B.R., Financial Appraisal of State Ware-Housing Corporation: A Case Study of Rajasthan Ware, Housing Corporation, Jaipure: University of Rajasthan, July 1979, pp.3-4.
10. Kenndey, R.D. and McMuller, S.Y., Financial Statements- Forms, analysis and Interpretation, Illinois: Richard D.Irwin, 1952, p.17.
11. Hingorani, N.L. and Ramanathan, A.P., Management Accounting, New Delhi: S. Chand, 1994, p.92.
12. Sinkey, Joseph F., Jr., Commercial Bank Financial Management, New York: Maxwell Macmillan International, 1992, pp. 426-427.
13. Reed, Edward, M., Commercial Bank Management, New York: Harpet and Row Publishers, 1963, p. 525.
14. Helfert, E.A., Techniques of Financial Analysis, Illinois: Richard D. Irwin, 1972, p.53.
15. Kennedy, R.D., and McMuller, S.Y., Financial Statements – Forms, Analysis and Interpretation, IIlinois: Richard D. Irwin, 1968, p.418.
16. Pandey, I.M., Financial Management, Bombay: Vikas Publishing House Pvt. Ltd., 1979, pp.451-452.

CHAPTER–5

PATTERN OF FUNDS MOBILIZED BY THE SAMPLE BORROWERS.

INTRODUCTION

In the present Chapter the profile of the sample borrowers and the mobilization of funds by them have been described. Based on the profile of the applicants, the banks sanction loans. The profile of the applicant includes the age, social status, educational qualification, size of the family and monthly income of the sample borrowers. The bank provides loans after a detailed verification of the profile of the borrowers. Relevant information from the borrowers is very important to the banks while sanctioning the loans. Hence, in this Chapter, the profile of the borrowers has been discussed clearly. Funds mobilization by them for construction of houses has also been analyzed. Data have been gathered through schedules and personal interviews.

PROFILE OF THE SAMPLE BORROWERS

Commercial banks allot housing loans on the basis of two factors namely estimated cost and repayment procedure. About 330 sample borrowers belonging to 4 select banks have been classified on the basis of their age, social status, educational background, occupation, family size and monthly income of the borrower.

Age-Wise Classification

The house building activity is taken up by different individuals at different stages of life. So age forms an important aspect that is to be taken into consideration while sanctioning house loans. Normally, in a developing country like India,people start constructing their own houses after 30 years of age as they need sufficient time to save from their earlier earning. Table 1 shows the age-wise classification of sample borrowers.

Out of the total number of sample borrowers, the highest of 178 borrowers, constituting 53.94 per cent fall under the early age group of 30-40 years. About 5.45 per cent of housing loans are sanctioned to the borrowers with 50-60 years age. The banks perceive that in this age group people are about to retire, and their repaying capacity would come down. The sample borrowers belonging to the age group of 30-40 years of all sample bank branches are supposed to have a similar share in the total sample between 51.85 per cent and 55.0 per cent.

Table 1

Age-Wise Classification Of Sample Borrowers

Sample Banks	*Upto 30*	*30-40*	*40-50*	*50-60*	*Total*
SBI	19(12.67)	81(54.0)	42(28.0)	08(5.33)	150(100.0)
AB	18(16.98)	58(54.72)	24(22.64)	06(5.66)	106(100.0)
SB	11(20.37)	28(51.85)	12(22.22)	03(5.56)	54(100.0)
IB	03(15.0)	11(55.0)	05(25.0)	01(5.0)	20(100.0)
Total	51(15.45)	178(53.94)	83(25.15)	18(5.45)	330(100.0)

Chi – Square Value(X^2 - 20.75
Level of Significance (%)- 5
Degrees of Freedom- 9
Critical Value of Chi-Square - 16.919

Note: Figures in the parentheses indicate percentage to total
Source: Field Survey

For the age group of 40-50 years, it is observed that the percentage of loan sanctioning is almost similar in AB and SB. It ranges between 25.0 per cent and 28.0 per cent in IB and SBI respectively. For the age group of 50 to 60 years, it is observed that percentage of loan sanction is as low as 5 per cent. In SB, the maximum percentage of loans are sanctioned for the sample borrowers belonging upto 30 years age. It is observed that in all sample banks the maximum percentage of loans are sanctioned for the sample borrowers belonging to the age group of 30-40 years, as the sample borrowers of this age group posses repayment ability when compared with other age group. Chart 1 represents the age-wise classification of sample borrowers.

Chart 1: Age-Wise Classification of Sample Borrowers

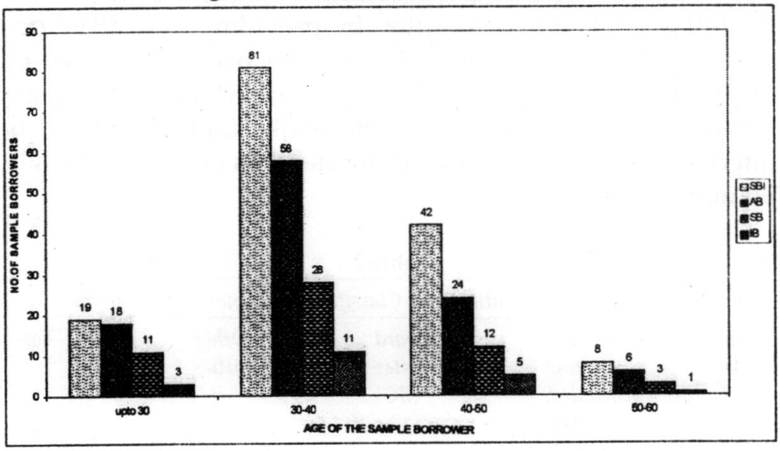

Hypothesis Formulated and Tested

It is presumed that *'there are no significant differences between select commercial banks and age of sample borrowers'*. The calculated value of Chi–Square Value (X^2) is 20.75 and the Table value at 5 per cent level of significance for 9 degrees of freedom is 16.919. The calculated value is greater than the critical value of X^2. Hence, the null hypothesis is rejected.

Social Status-wise Classification

Actually, the sample banks are not giving the house loans by giving any sort of importance of community. India has many religions and innumerable communities. Table 2 shows the social status-wise classification of sample borrowers.

neue. Die Abbildungen des Rup-Speichers pauste sie zum Teil ab, verband die einzelnen Bestandteile jedoch willkürlich miteinander.

Sie schafften vier Seiten, bis die Eltern heimkamen. Das musste für ihre Täuschung genügen. Kion verstaute die Originale unterm Bett. Während Rup und Lara in der Küche hantierten, eilte er nach nebenan, um die Fälschungen zu platzieren.

Fabia blieb im Zimmer zurück. Taten sie das Richtige? Doch sie sagte nichts. Dafür war sie viel zu aufgeregt.

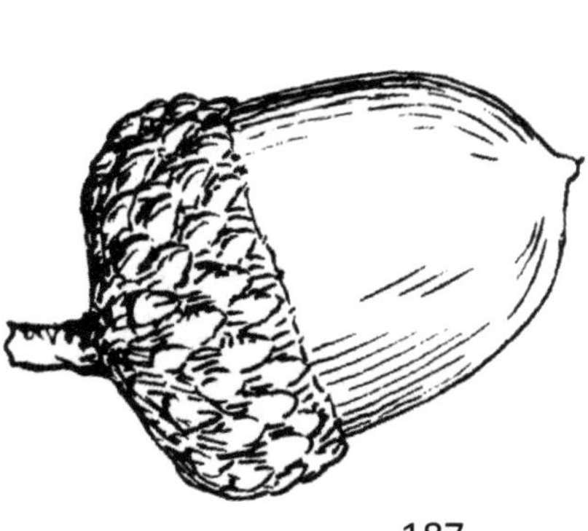

Out of the total sample, other category (OC) has started about 60 per cent and BC, SC/ST category put-together constitute about below 40 per cent. The least percentage of sample borrowers are from SC/ST category when compared to others. It varied between 2 per cent and 12 per cent in all the banks selected for the study. Bank-wise analysis reveals that SB has given top priority to SC and ST by giving 11.11 per cent of its housing loans. SBI has the least place by giving only 8 per cent of its loans to this category. In the case of BC category also, SB has given more loans i.e., 35.19 per cent, which is the highest share when compared to that of other banks. Here also, the SBI has taken least position by providing only 28.67 per cent of its housing loans to the BC category. In the case of other category, SBI's share is 63.33 per cent, which is the highest when compared to other sample banks under study. It is inferred from that SBI has concentrated less on SC/STs, while SB more on SC/STs and BC's.

Table 2

Social Status-Wise Classification of Sample Borrowers

Sample Banks	*Scheduled Castes/ Scheduled Tribes (SC/ST)*	*Backward Castes (BC)*	*Other Communities*	*Total*
SBI	12(8.0)	43(28.67)	95(63.33)	150(100.0)
AB	09(8.49)	35(33.02)	62(58.49)	106(100.0)
SB	06(11.11)	19(35.19)	29(53.70)	54(100.0)
IB	02(10.0)	07(35.0)	11(55.0)	20(100.0)
Total	29(8.79)	104(31.51)	197(59.70)	330(100.0)

Chi – Square Value (X^2) - 2.02
Level of Significance (%) - 5
Degrees of Freedom - 6
Critical Value of Chi-Square - 12.592

Note: Figures in the parentheses indicate percentage to total
Source: Field survey

Chart 2 shows the social status-wise classification of sample borrowers.

Chart 2: Social Status-Wise Classification of Sample Borrowers

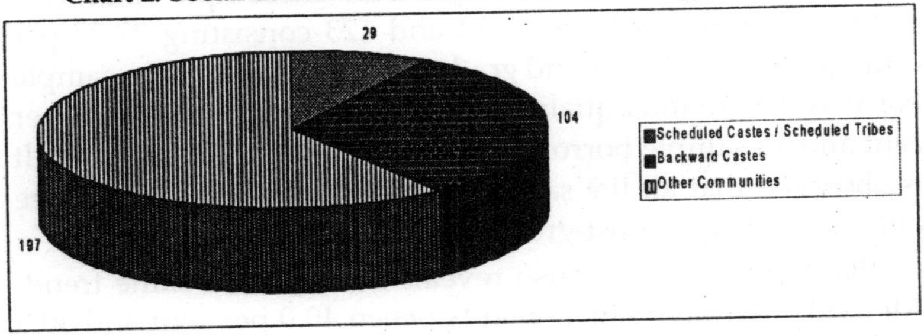

Hypothesis Formulated and Tested

It is presupposed that *'there are no significant differences between select commercial banks and social status of sample borrowers'*. The calculated value of Chi-Square Value (X^2) (2.02) is less than the Table value (12.592) at 5 per cent level of significance for 6 degrees of freedom. Hence, the null hypothesis is accepted.

Educational Background-wise Classification

Educational background is closely related to the earnings of sample borrowers. It is relevant to study the impact of educational qualification on availing housing loans from banks. Details of educational qualifications of the sample borrowers are shown in Table 3.

Table 3

Educational Background-Wise Classification of Sample Borrowers

Sample Bank	*Metric*	*Intermediate*	*Graduates*	*Post-Graduates*	*Total*
SBI	08(5.33)	12(8.00)	62(41.33)	68(45.33)	150(100.0)
AB	06(5.66)	11(10.37)	40(37.74)	49(46.23)	106(100.0)
SB	04(7.41)	09(16.67)	18(33.33)	23(42.59)	54(100.0)
IB	01(5.00)	04(20.00)	03(15.00)	12(60.00)	20(100.0)
Total	19(5.76)	36(10.91)	123(37.27)	152(46.06)	330(100.0)

Chi – Square Value (X^2) - 12.71
Level of Significance (%) - 5
Degrees of Freedom - 9
Critical Value of Chi-Square - 16.919

Note: Figures in the parentheses indicate percentage to total
Source: Field survey

As seen from the Table, out of total 330 sample borrowers 152 constituting 46.06 per cent and 123 consisting 37.27 per cent are post-graduates and graduates respectively. The sample borrowers with inter qualification are 36 constituting 10.91 per cent and 19 sample borrowers are metric with 5.76 per cent. It is observed that all the sample banks sanctioned major share of house loans for post-graduate holders.

Bank-wise analysis also reveals more or less same trend. All the banks have sanctioned between 40.0 per cent and 50.0 per cent of loans to post graduates. IB has sanctioned highest share of 60.0 per cent of loans to post-graduates. Second priority was given to graduates in all the sample banks by sanctioning between 30.0 per cent and 41.0 per cent of loans. But in the case of IB graduates stood at third place by getting 15.0 per cent of loans only. The share of loans to intermediate varied between 8.0 per cent and 20.0 per cent in all the banks by occupying third position with the exception of IB. And less than 10 per cent of loans were providing to matriculates. It is, thus, inferred that all the sample banks have sanctioned the loans by giving priority to higher education. In other words, sample borrowers with higher qualifications were given top priority while lower qualifications lesser importance. Chart 3 represents the educational background-wise classifications of sample borrowers.

Chart 3: Educational Background-wise Classification of Sample Borrowers

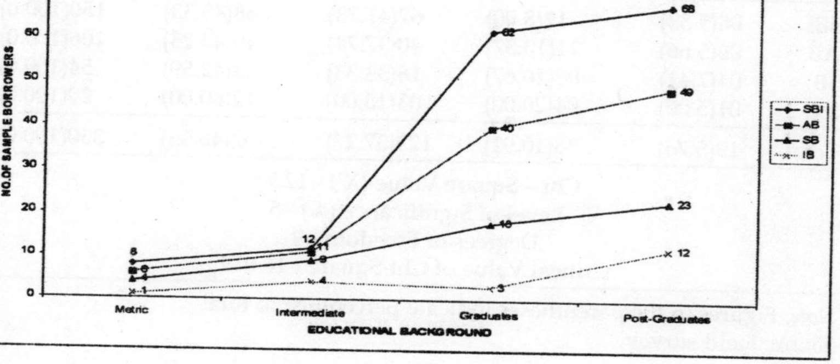

Hypothesis Formulated and Tested

It is hypothesised that *'there are no significant differences between select commercial banks and educational qualifications of sample borrowers'*. The calculated Chi-Square Value (X^2) (12.71) is less than the Table value (16.919) at 5 per cent level of significance for 9 degrees of freedom. Thus, the null hypothesis is accepted.

Occupation-wise Classification

Occupation is the main source of income for every individual. Due to increase in occupational income, there will be corresponding increase in savings. This will be considered while sanctioning of loans by the bank branches. Table 4 manifests occupation-wise classification of sample borrower.

Among all the occupations, employees have taken the highest share of loans i.e., 72.12 per cent, followed by business and agriculture with 24.55 per cent and 3.33 per cent respectively. Bank-wise data also reveals the same pattern. All the banks have given top priority for employees by sanctioning between 70.0 per cent and 75.0 per cent of total loans. The share of business people varied in between 20.0 per cent and 26.0 per cent.

Table 4

Occupation-Wise Classification Of Sample Borrowers

(in Nos.)

Sample Bank	*Employee*	*Business*	*Agriculture*	*Total*
SBI	106(70.67)	39(26.0)	05(3.33)	150(100.0)
AB	79(74.53)	24(22.64)	03(2.83)	106(100.0)
SB	38(70.37)	14(25.93)	02(3.70)	54(100.0)
IB	15(75.0)	04(20.0)	01(5.00)	20(100.0)
Total	238(72.12)	81(24.55)	11(3.33)	330(100.0)

Chi - Square Value(X^2) - 2.65
Level of Significance (%) - 5
Degrees of Freedom - 6
Critical Value of Chi-Square - 12.592

Note: Figures in the parentheses indicate percentage to total
Source: Field survey

A very least percentage of loans have been sanctioned to agriculturists. It is only less than 5.0 per cent. The reason might be that employees have fixed income source and the banks can deduct their loan installments at source itself. In case of business also, there is higher repaying capacity. But the income of agriculturists is completely uncertain. So, banks have given least priority to agriculturists. Occupation-wise classification of sample borrowers is depicted in Chart 4.

Chart 4: Occupation-wise Classification of Sample Borrowers

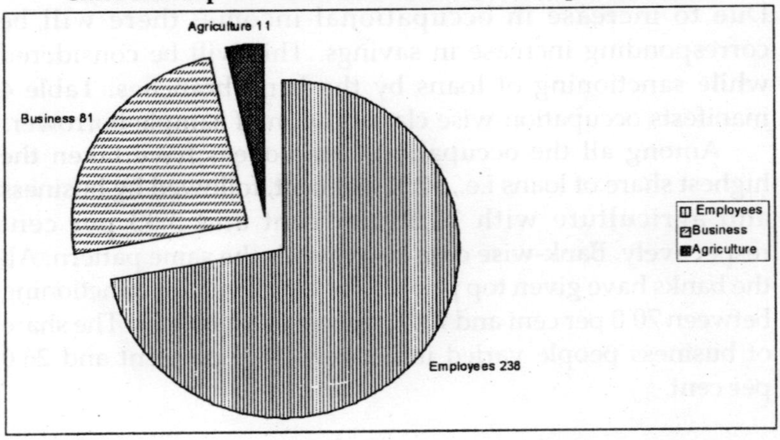

Hypothesis Formulated and Tested

It is presupposed that *'there are no significant differences between select commercial banks and occupation of sample borrowers'*. It is evident that the calculated value of Chi – Square Value (X^2) (2.65)and the Table value (12.592) at 5 per cent level of significance for 6 degree of freedom. The calculated value is less than the Table value. Hence, the null hypothesis is accepted.

Family Size–wise Classification

The size of the family directly impacts the savings and expenditure of individuals. Larger the size of the family more will be the expenditure and lesser will be the scope for savings. Family size forms one of the important basic factors on the basis of which the house loans is fixed. The scope of savings completely depends on the expenditure of the family size. The savings are then utilized to some extent in the construction of house. Hence, classification of family size becomes relevant. Family size-wise classification of sample borrowers is portrayed in Table 5.

Table 5

Family Size-Wise Classification of Sample Borrowers
(in number)

Sample Bank	*Upto 3*	*3-4*	*4-5*	*5-6*	*6-7*	*Total*
SBI	29(19.33)	44(29.33)	51(34.0)	14(9.33)	12(8.0)	150(100.0)
AB	19(17.92)	34(32.08)	35(33.02)	08(7.55)	10(9.43)	106(100.0)
SB	06(11.11)	19(35.19)	22(40.74)	04(7.41)	03(5.56)	54(100.0)
IB	03(15.0)	10(50.0)	04(20.0)	02(10.0)	01(5.0)	20(100.0)
Total	57(17.27)	108(32.42)	112(33.94)	28(8.48)	26(7.88)	330(100.0)

Chi – Square Value (X^2) - 9.44
Level of Significance (%) - 5
Degrees of Freedom - 12
Critical Value of Chi-Square - 21.026

Note: Figures in the parentheses indicate percentage to total
Source: Field survey

As seen from the Table, out of 330 sample borrowers from all sample banks, family-size group consisting of 4 to 5 member has taken the highest percentage, of loans 33.94 followed by the size of 3-4 member size group with 32.42 per cent. The family-size consisting of upto 3 members has taken 17.27 per cent and the family size where 6-7 members have taken only 7.88 per cent of house loans.

Individual bank analysis also reveals the same trend except IB, all the three other branches i.e., SBI, AB, SB have given priority to the family size of 4 to 5 members by sanctioning 34.0, 33.02 and 40.74 per cent of loans respectively. In the case of IB share of this family size group is only 20.0 per cent and the family size of 3-4 members is given higher priority by giving 50.0 per cent of loans. Banks individually have also given less importance to large family size. Chart 5 shows the family size-wise classification of sample borrowers.

Chart 5: Family Size-wise Classification of Sample Borrowers

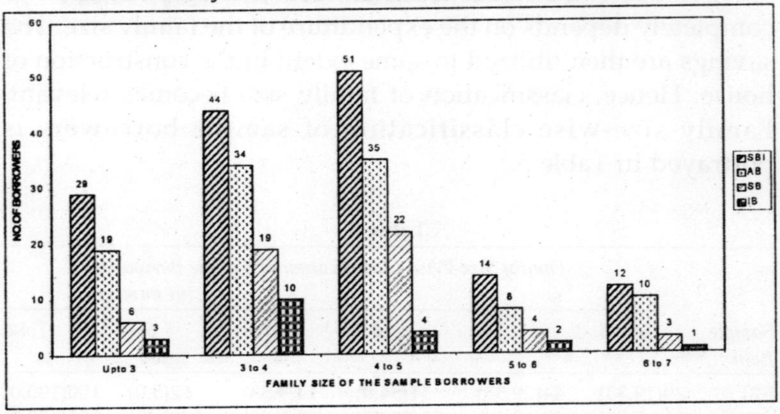

Hypothesis Formulated and Tested

It is hypothesised formulated that '*there are no significant differences between select commercial banks and size of the family sample borrowers*'.

It is observed that the calculated Chi–Square Value (X^2) (9.44) is less than the Table value (21.026) at 5 per cent level of significance for 12 degrees of freedom. Hence, a null hypothesis is accepted.

Monthly Income–wise Classification

At the time of sanctioning the house loans the banks must see monthly income of the loanees. To apply for house loan, the borrowers must have regular monthly income. On the basis of monthly income, the sample borrowers are divided into four categories; upto Rs. 10000, Rs. 10000-15000, and Rs. 15000-20000 and above Rs. 20000. monthly income-wise classification of sample borrowers are presented in Table 6.

It is evident that sample banks have given high priority while sanctioning the loans to the sample borrowers who fall under the monthly income category of Rs. 10000-15000 by giving 42.42 per cent of total loans to this group, followed by Rs. 15000-20000 and above Rs. 20000 with 30.0 per cent and 22.42 per cent respectively.

Table 6

Monthly Income-Wise Classification of the Sample Borrowers
(in number)

Sample Bank	*Upto 10000*	*10000-15000*	*15000-20000*	*Above 20000*	*Total*
SBI	09(6.0)	59(39.33)	48(32.0)	34(22.67)	150(100.0)
AB	05(4.72)	44(41.51)	32(30.19)	25(23.58)	106(100.0)
SB	03(5.56)	26(48.15)	13(24.07)	12(22.22)	54(100.0)
IB	-	11(55.0)	06(30.0)	03(15.0)	20(100.0)
Total	17(5.15)	140(42.42)	99(30.0)	74(22.42)	330(100.0)

Calculated 'ANOVA' Value - 7.08
Level of Significance (%) - 5.0
Critical Value of 'ANOVA' - 3.59

Note: Figures in the parentheses indicate percentage to total
Source: Field survey

Individually, all the sample bank branches followed the same pattern. Highest percentage of loans have gone to the income groups of Rs.10000-15000. IB and SB have given more than half of the loans, i.e., 55.0 per cent and 48.15 per cent to this category. All the sample banks have given lesser share of loans to the respondents fall under the group upto Rs.10000. It can be inferred that fear of non-recovery of loans from low income group might have been the reason for less importance to low income group and high income group might not have approached the bank for house loans. Monthly income-wise classification of the sample borrowers is shown in Chart 6.

Chart 6: Monthly Income-wise Classification of the Sample Borrowers

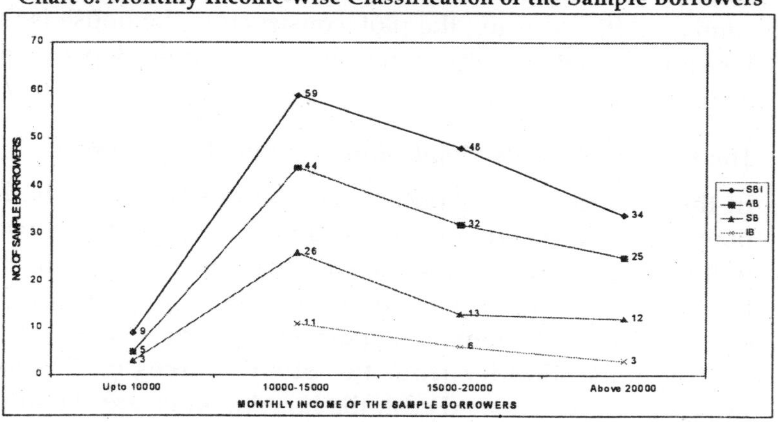

Hypothesis Formulated and Tested

It is presumed that *'there are no significant differences between select commercial banks and monthly income of sample borrowers'.*

It is found that 'ANOVA' calculated value 1.91 is less than the Table value 3.59 of sample banks at 5 per cent level of significance for (3,11) degrees of freedom. Thus, the null hypothesis is accepted.

FUNDS MOBILIZATION BY SAMPLE BORROWERS

After analyzing the profile of the sample borrowers, pattern of mobilization of the funds by them for the construction of houses is observed. Every sample borrowers major task is mobilization of funds for house construction as funds mobilization is the most crucial aspect in housing activity, which is the capital intensive in nature. Most of the problems of the sample borrowers are related to the funds mobilization activity. Hence, the pattern of funds mobilization is an important aspect in any study of housing finance

Funds Mobilization for Securing House Plot

To construct a house, any individual has to first acquire a suitable plot. He/She may purchase the plot either through informal sources like, personal savings or taking the money from money lenders or others (friends, relatives etc) or formal sources like financial institutions or inherit from ancestral sources. After securing the plot, constructing the house is the foremost activity. In this connection, he mainly depends on external sources.

The Pattern of Funds Mobilization by Sample Borrowers

In the construction of houses, first the estimated cost is the main issue. Depending on the estimated cost, the borrower will decide the amount of loans to apply for. In general, the banks will sanction upto a maximum of 85 per cent of the estimated cost. The remaining portion is supposed to be taped by the house builder from the other sources of finance. Depending on estimated cost, the housing units are classified into five categories on the basis of estimated cost viz., upto Rs.2 lakhs; Rs. 2-4 lakhs; Rs.4-6 lakhs; Rs. 6-8 lakhs and above Rs.8 lakhs.

Mobilization of Funds by State Bank of India Sample Group

Table 7 captures the pattern of funds mobilization by the borrowers of SBI.

Out of the total funds required for construction of houses in all the categories, the share of informal sources of funds is more than the formal sources. About 54.59 per cent of funds are from informal and 45.41 per cent of funds are from formal sources i.e., from SBI. In the informal category also, funds from personal savings are more with 42.92 per cent. A meagre funds are mobilized from money lenders and others with 9.44 per cent and 2.23 per cent respectively. SBI has given more loans of 54.93 per cent to the housing units where the investment is Rs.8 to 12 lakhs. In the remaining categories percentage of funds from SBI is around 45 per cent. Personal savings played a key role in the construction of house in all investment categories. The coefficient of correlation (r) between total of informal sources and formal sources is 0.91. Hence, it may be concluded that two variables viz., informal sources and formal sources are positively correlated.

Mobilization of Funds by Andhra Bank Sample Group

Mobilization of funds by the sample borrowers of AB is embodied in Table 8. Out of total funds required for the construction of housing units the share of informal sources of funds is just more than the formal sources. About 50.34 per cent of funds are secured from the informal sources and 49.66 per cent of funds are procured from AB. In informal sources, only 11.21 per cent of funds contributed from money lenders and other sources and the share of personal savings is more with 39.13 per cent.

With regard to number of units, the highest of 41 units are in the range of Rs.2 to 4 lakhs of investment. For the AB, estimated cost is not the criteria to sanction the loans as it

Table 7

Sources of Housing Finance to SBI Sample Borrowers in Relation to Estimated Cost

(Rs.in lakhs)

Estimated Cost Group (Rs.)	*Informal Sources*					
	Personal Savings 1	*Money Lenders 2*	*Others 3*	*Total 4=1+2+3*	*SBI 5*	*Total Actual Cost 6=4+5*
Upto 2(28 units)	18.26(34.95)	8.12(15.54)	2.35(4.50)	28.73(55.0)	23.51(45.0)	52.24(100.0)
2-4(40 units)	68.91(43.10)	12.06(7.54)	6.96(4.35)	87.93(54.99)	71.94(44.0)	159.87(100.0)
4-6(43 units)	128.58(40.06)	39.27(12.24)	8.68(2.70)	176.53(55.0)	144.43(45.0)	320.96(100.0)
6-8(27 units)	148.27(52.95)	18.73(6.69)	1.0(0.36)	168.0(60.0)	112.0(40.0)	280.00(100.0)
8 above (12 units)	63.12(34.64)	15.77(8.65)	3.24(1.78)	82.13(45.07)	100.10(54.93)	182.23(100.0)
Total (150units)	427.14(42.92)	93.95(9.44)	22.23 (2.23)	543.32(54.59)	451.98(45.41)	995.30(100.0)

Coefficient of Correlation (r)= 0.91

Note: Figures in the parentheses indicate percentages to total
Source: Field survey

Table 8

Sources of Housing Finance to AB Sample Borrowers in Relation to Estimated Cost

(Rs.in lakhs)

	Informal Sources					
Estimated Cost Group (Rs.)	*Personal Savings 1*	*Money Lenders 2*	*Others 3*	*Total 4=1+2+3*	*AB 5*	*Total Actual Cost 6=4+5*
Upto 2(16units)	16.46 (35.54)	6.27(13.53)	2.75(5.94)	25.48(55.01)	20.84 (44.99)	46.32(100.0)
2-4(41 units)	76.22 (41.72)	18.36 (10.05)	2.55 (1.40)	97.13(53.17)	85.54 (46.83)	182.67(100.0)
4-6(25 units)	72.76 (37.07)	12.29 (6.26)	3.27 (1.67)	88.32(45.0)	107.95(55.0)	196.27 (100.0)
6-8(19units)	62.15 (40.44)	18.34 (11.93)	2.81 (1.83)	83.30(54.20)	70.38 (45.80)	153.68(100.0)
8 above (5 units)	19.42(37.09)	4.14 (7.91)	-	23.56(45.0)	28.80 (55.0)	52.36(100.0)
Total (106 units)	247.01 (39.13)	59.40 (9.41)	11.38 (1.80)	317.79(50.34)	313.51 (49.66)	631.30(100.0)

Coefficient of Correlation (r)= 0.79

Note: Figures in the parentheses indicate percentages to total
Source: Field survey

did not sanction any loan based on the estimated cost. The share of AB is more or less 50 per cent in all the categories of estimated cost. On an average, informal sources have played a vital role in the construction of houses in all categories. It is found that there is a positive co-efficient of correlation between informal sources and formal sources is 0.79.

Mobilization of Funds by Syndicate Bank Sample Group

The details of sources of funds by SB sample group in relation to estimate cost is depicted in Table 9.

Out of the total funds required for the construction of housing units by the sample borrowers of SB, the contribution of informal sources is higher than the formal (SB) sources. The total informal sources contribute 50.89 per cent of fund and 49.11 per cent of funds have been borrowed from SB. Among the informal sources, funds raised from personal savings are more with 41.46 per cent and funds secured from money lenders and others with 7.58 per cent and 1.85 per cent respectively. In the formal sources, SB has provided highest share of loans (57.49 per cent) to the housing units where the estimated cost is above Rs.8 lakhs followed by 52.80 per cent to Rs.6-8 lakhs category, 48.26 per cent to Rs.2-4 lakhs category and 47.0 per cent and 44.99 per cent to Rs.4-6 lakhs and upto Rs.2 lakhs categories respectively. While sanctioning the loans, SB has given priority to the range of estimated cost. It increases the amount of loan with the increase of estimated cost. In the informal sources, personal savings played a major role. There is a positive relationship between informal sources and funds from SB as the coefficient of correlation (r) 0.93.

Mobilization of funds by Indian Bank sample group

Table 10 provides the details of funds mobilization by borrowers of SB in relation to the estimated cost. All the 20 sample borrowers in IB have procured loans through both informal and bank sources. The contribution of informal source is 51.87 per cent and formal sources in 48.13 per cent. It is observed that in the informal sources, the share of personal

Table 9

Sources of Housing Finance to SB Sample Borrowers in Relation to Estimated Cost

(Rs.in lakhs)

Estimated Cost Group (Rs.)	*Informal Sources*					
	Personal Savings 1	*Money Lenders 2*	*Others 3*	*Total 4=1+2+3*	*SB 5*	*Total Actual Cost 6=4+5*
Upto 2(9units)	8.32(38.62)	2.26 (10.49)	1.27 (5.90)	11.85(55.01)	9.69(44.99)	21.54(100.0)
2-4(26 units)	54.56(44.46)	6.24(5.08)	2.70(2.20)	63.50(51.74)	59.23(48.26)	122.73(100.0)
4-6(12 units)	38.49(43.11)	8.83(9.89)	-	47.32(53.0)	41.96(47.0)	89.28(100.0)
6-8(5units)	18.32(34.81)	4.78 (9.08)	1.74(3.31)	24.84(47.20)	27.79(52.80)	52.63(100.0)
8 above (2 units)	8.17 (36.75)	1.28(5.76)	-	9.45(42.51)	12.78(57.49)	22.23(100.0)
Total (54 units)	127.86(41.46)	23.39(7.58)	5.71(1.85)	156.96(50.89)	151.45(49.11)	308.41(100.0)

Coefficient of Correlation (r) = 0.93

Note: Figures in the parentheses indicate percentages to total
Source: Field survey

Table 10
Sources of Housing Finance to IB Sample Borrowers in Relation to Estimated Cost

(Rs.in lakhs)

	Informal Sources					
Estimated Cost Group (Rs. Lakhs)	*Personal Savings 1*	*Money Lenders 2*	*Others 3*	*Total 4=1+2+3*	*IB 5*	*Total Actual Cost 6=4+5*
Upto 2(3units)	1.62(34.61)	0.95(20.30)	-	2.57 (54.91)	2.11 (45.09)	4.68(100.0)
2-4(13 units)	25.26(37.56)	8.32(12.37)	3.41(5.07)	36.99(55.0)	30.27(45.0)	67.26(100.0)
4-6(4 units)	9.72(29.64)	4.28(13.05)	0.76(2.32)	14.76(45.01)	18.03(54.99)	32.79(100.0)
6-8	-	-	-	-	-	-
8 above	-	-	-	-	-	-
Total (20 units)	36.60(34.95)	13.55(12.94)	4.17(3.98)	54.32(51.87)	50.41(48.13)	104.73(100.0)

Note: Figures in the parentheses indicate percentages to total
Source: Field survey

savings is more with 34.95 per cent followed money lenders with 12.94 per cent and other sources with 3.98 per cent only. Of all sample banks, IB has sanctioned more loans to the housing units in the category of Rs.4-6 lakhs with 54.99 per cent followed by upto Rs.2 lakhs and Rs.2-4 lakhs with 45.09 per cent and 45.0 per cent respectively. It is also noticed that IB has not given any loans to the housing units of Rs.6-8 lakhs and above Rs.8 lakhs categories.

It is clear that personal savings have played an important role in securing funds from informal sources for housing construction by sample borrowers.

Aggregate Pattern in Total Sample Group

Contribution of funds from different sources of housing finance by all sample borrowers is presented in Table 11. All the 330 sample borrowers have procured funds both form the formal and informal sources. Funds from formal sources are less than the informal sources. Funds from formal sources is 47.43 per cent (Rs.967.35 lakhs) out of the total estimated cost of Rs.2039.74 lakhs. The contribution of informal sources such as personal savings, money lenders and others is 52.57 per cent (1072.39lakhs). Out of all the informal sources, the share of personal savings is more with 41.11per cent followed by money lenders and others with 9.33 per cent and 2.13 per cent respectively.

Contribution from informal sources is more with 3 per cent to 10 per cent in all the estimated cost categories except where the estimated cost is above Rs.8 lakhs. It is understood that sample banks have given priority to the high cost of houses. The percentage of loan in low cost units i.e., upto Rs.2 lakhs is 45.99 and in high cost units i.e., above Rs.8 lakhs is 55.17 per cent. The coefficient of correlation (r) between informal sources and funds from sample banks is 0.96. Hence, it may be concluded that two variables of total informal sources and funds by select banks are positively correlated. Chart 7 represents the sources of housing finance to total sample borrowers in relation to estimated cost.

Table 11

Sources of Housing Finance for Total Sample Borrowers in Relation to Estimated Cost

(Rs.in lakhs)

	Informal Sources					
Estimated Cost Group (Rs.)	*Personal Savings 1*	*Money Lenders 2*	*Others 3*	*Total 4=1+2+3*	*Sample Banks 5*	*Total Actual Cost 6=4+5*
Upto 2(56units)	44.66(35.79)	17.60(14.10)	6.37(5.10)	68.63(55.0)	56.15(45.0)	124.78(100.0)
2-4 (120 units)	224.95(42.24)	44.98(8.45)	15.62(2. 93)	285.55(53.62)	246.98(46.38)	532.53(100.0)
4-6(84 units)	249.55(39.03)	64.67(10.12)	12.71(1.99)	326.93(51.14)	312.37(48.86)	639.30(100.0)
6-8(51units)	228.74(47.03)	41.85(8.61)	5.55(1.14)	276.14(56.78)	210.17(43.22)	486.31(100.0)
8 above (19 units)	90.71(35.32)	21.19(8.25)	3.24(1.26)	115.14(44.83)	141.68(55.17)	256.82(100.0)
Total (330 units)	838.61(41.11)	190.29(9.33)	43.49(2.13)	1072.39(52.57)	967.35(47.43)	2039.74(100.0)

Correlation Coefficient (r) = 0.96

Note: Figures in the parentheses indicate percentages to total
Source: Field survey

Chart 7: Sources of Housing Finance for Total Sample Borrowers in Relation to Estimated Cost

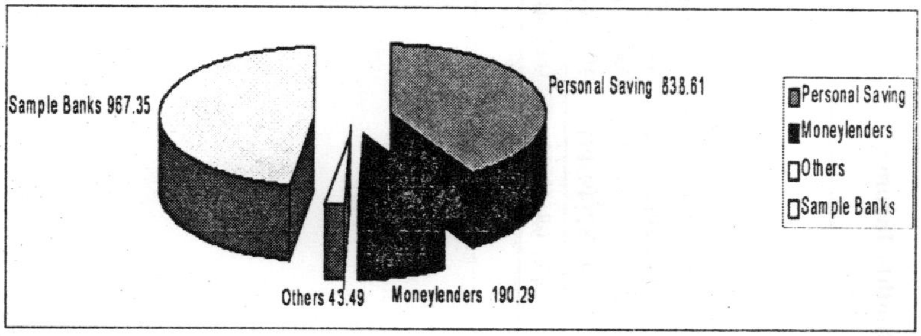

Funds Mobilization in Relation to Monthly Income of Sample Borrowers

Commercial bank branches mainly consider the monthly income of the borrowers while sanctioning housing loans. All sample banks recover loans in monthly installments from the sample borrowers. In general, the term monthly loan installment is a normal condition. The select banks collect monthly loan installments upto 30 per cent to 40 per cent of the monthly income of the borrowers. Even the estimated cost of the house construction depends on the monthly income of the borrowers. In this context, the pattern of funds mobilization in relation to the monthly income of the housing loan borrowers is analyzed. All the sample borrowers are classified into four categories on the basis of their monthly income viz., upto Rs.10000, between Rs.10000-15000, between Rs.15000-20000 and as above Rs.20000.

Mobilization of Funds by State Bank of India Sample Group

Sources of housing finance to SBI sample group in relation to monthly income are depicted in Table 12.

Out of the total funds required for the construction of houses in all categories, the percentage of informal sources of funds is 54.59 and the percentage share from SBI is 45.41. It is clear that SBI has given 49.61 per cent of loans to the borrowers whose monthly income is upto Rs.10000 followed by monthly income of above Rs.20000 with 46.30 per cent. It is observed that SBI has not given any priority to the high income

Table 12

Sources of Housing Finance to SBI Sample Borrowers in Relation to Monthly Income

(Rs.in lakhs)

Monthly Income (Rs.)	*Informal Sources*					
	Personal Savings 1	*Money Lenders 2*	*Others 3*	*Total 4=1+2+3*	*SBI 5*	*Total Actual Cost 6=4+5*
Upto 10000(9units)	19.84(39.50)	3.91(7.78)	1.56(3.11)	25.31(50.39)	24.92(49.61)	50.23(100.0)
10000-15000(59 units)	222.34(43.16)	42.17(8.19)	12.12(2.35)	276.63(53.70)	238.49(46.30)	515.12(100.0)
15000-20000(48units)	101.69(42.67)	37.11(15.57)	5.79(2.43)	144.59(60.67)	93.75(39.33)	238.34. (100.0)
Above 20000(34 units)	83.27(43.45)	10.76(5.62)	2.76(1.44)	96.79(50.51)	94.82(49.49)	191.61(100.0)
Total (150 units)	427.14(42.92)	93.95(9.44)	22.23(2.23)	543.32(54.59)	451.98(45.41)	995.30(100.0)

Correlation Coefficient (r)= 0.99

Note: Figures in the parentheses indicate percentages to total
Source: Field survey

households while sanctioning the house loans. In the informal category, personal savings dominates all the other informal sources. The share of personal savings is 42.92 per cent followed by money lenders and others with 9.44 per cent and 2.23 per cent respectively. Coefficient of correlation (r) is positively correlated between informal sources and a formal source is 0.99.

Mobilization of Funds by Andhra Bank Sample Group

Details of mobilization of funds by sample borrowers of AB are given in Table 13. It is clear that in AB also the percentage share of informal sources is marginally high with 0.68 per cent. In the informal category, funds from personal savings have taken lion's share with 39.13 per cent. Only less than 10.0 per cent of funds are contributed from money lenders and others. Out of the total 106 sample units, only five units fall in the income category of upto Rs.10000. And the highest of 44 units are fund in the category of Rs. 10000-15000 and highest amount of Rs.160.09 lakhs has been sanctioned to this category. The number of units have started to decrease when income increases. It means that bank has given much priority to the lower income people. In the high income category, less number of customers might have approached the bank for housing loans.

Contribution of funds from personal savings is more in the income categories. The coefficient of correlation(r) between informal sources and formal sources is 0.98.

Mobilization of Funds by Syndicate Bank Sample Group

Details of pattern of funds in SB are given in Table 14. All 54 sample group are classified into four categories based on their monthly income. Out of the total Rs.308.41 lakhs of sanctions for 54 sample housing units, 50.89 per cent (Rs.156.96 lakhs) is contributed from informal sources and 49.11 per cent (Rs.151.45 lakhs) is secured from formal sources i.e., SB. In SB also, the share of funds from informal sources are comparatively more. Out of 50.89 per cent (Rs.156.96 lakhs) from informal source,

Table 13

Sources of Housing Finance to AB Sample Borrowers in Relation to Monthly Income

(Rs.in lakhs)

Monthly Income (in Rs.)	*Informal Sources*				*AB*	*Total Actual*
	Personal Savings 1	*Money Lenders 2*	*Others 3*	*Total 4=1+2+3*	*5*	*Cost 6=4+5*
Upto 10000(5units)	22.65(30.88)	7.51(10.24)	1.0(1.36)	31.16(42.49)	42.18(57.51)	73.34(100.0)
10000-15000(44 units)	132.89(42.10)	18.17(5.75)	4.50(1.43)	155.56(49.28)	160.09(50.72)	315.65(100.0)
15000-20000(32 units)	55.17(39.40)	15.56(11.11)	3.86(2.75)	74.59(53.26)	65.45(46.74)	140.04(100.0)
Above 20000(25 units)	36.30(35.49)	18.16(17.76)	2.02(1.98)	56.48(55.23)	45.79(44.77)	102.27(100.0)
Total (106units)	247.01(39.13)	59.40(9.41)	11.38(1.80)	317.79(50.34)	313.51(49.66)	631.30(100.0)
Correlation Coefficient = 0.98						

Note: Figures in the parentheses indicate percentages to total
Source: Field survey

Table 14

Sources of Housing Finance to SB Sample Borrowers in Relation to Monthly Income

(Rs.in lakhs)

Monthly Income (Rs.)	*Informal Sources*					
	Personal Savings 1	*Money Lenders 2*	*Others 3*	*Total 4=1+2+3*	*SB 5*	*Total Actual Cost 6=4+5*
Upto 10000(3 units)	5.25(19.26)	3.19(11.70)	0.95(3.48)	9.39(34.44)	17.87(65.55)	27.26(100.0)
10000-15000(26 units)	76.89(44.66)	10.28(5.97)	2.10(1.22)	89.27(51.85)	82.89(48.15)	172.16(100.0)
15000-20000(13 units)	22.78(44.52)	2.93(5.73)	1.42(2.77)	27.13(53.02)	24.04(46.98)	51.17(100.0)
Above 20000(12 units)	22.94(39.74)	6.99(12.11)	1.24(2.16)	31.17(54.01)	26.65(46.09)	57.82(100.0)
Total (54 units)	127.86(41.46)	23.39(7.58)	5.71(1.85)	156.96(50.89)	151.45(49.11)	308.41(100.0)
Correlation Coefficient (r)= 0.99						

Note: Figures in the parentheses indicate percentages to total
Source: Field survey

41.46 per cent (Rs.127.86 lakhs) is raised from personal savings only. A meagre percentage of funds are raised from money lenders and others.

It is further observed that SB has also given more loans to the borrowers whose monthly income is between Rs.10000-15000. Maximum of 26 units are financed by SB in this income range. Only three units have been financed in the monthly income range of upto Rs.10000. And higher income groups are given less priority. About 46.98 per cent and 46.09 per cent of total sources are financed in the monthly income range of Rs.15000-20000 and above Rs.20000 respectively. Highest of 48.15 per cent (Rs.82.89 lakhs) of loans are given to the monthly income group of Rs.10000-15000. This is more than half of the total loans sanctioned to the sample housing units by SB. It is inferred that SB has also concentrated more on middle income group. Further more, the customers of SB have secured slightly higher percentage of funds from informal sources than formal sources. The coefficient correlation (r) between total of informal sources and formal sources is 0.99. Hence, it may be concluded that two variables total of informal sources and funds from SB are positively correlated.

Mobilization of Funds by Indian Bank Sample Group

The mobilization of funds by sample group of IB is depicted in the Table 15.

Out of the total funds required for the construction of houses in all categories, the percentage of informal sources of fund is 51.87 per cent and the share of IB is 48.13 per cent. IB has provided more share of (47.99 per cent) funds to the monthly income group of Rs.10000-15000Followed by the group of Rs.15000-20000 and above Rs.20000 with 49.19 per cent and 44.52 per cent respectively. It is also noticed that IB has not only given any loans to the borrowers whose monthly income is upto Rs.10000. In this paradigm, when observed in informal sources, the share of personal savings is more to that of funds from money lenders and others which are only 12.94 per cent and 3.98 per cent respectively.

Table 15

Sources of Housing Finance to IB Sample Borrowers in Relation to Monthly Income

(Rs.in lakhs)

Monthly Income (in Rs.)	*Informal Sources*					
	Personal Savings 1	*Money Lenders 2*	*Others 3*	*Total 4=1+2+3*	*IB 5*	*Total Actual Cost 6=4+5*
Upto 10000(-)	-	-	-	-	-	-
10000-15000(11 units)	23.65(34.63)	9.15(13.40)	2.72(3.98)	35.52(52.01)	32.78(47.99)	68.30(100.0)
15000-20000(6 units)	10.97(36.29)	3.18(10.52)	1.21(4.00)	15.36(50.81)	14.87(49.19)	30.23(100.0)
Above 20000(3units)	1.98(31.93)	1.22(19.68)	0.24(3.87)	3.44(55.48)	2.76(44.52)	6.20(100.0)
Total (20 units)	36.60(34.95)	13.55(12.94)	4.17(3.98)	54.32(51.87)	50.41(48.13)	104.73(100.0)

Note: Figures in the parentheses indicate percentages to total

Source: Field survey

Table 16

Sources of Housing Finance to Total Sample Borrowers in Relation to Monthly Income

(Rs.in lakhs)

Monthly Family Income	*Informal Sources* Personal Savings 1	Money Lenders 2	Others 3	Total 4=1+2+3	Sample Banks 5	Total Actual Cost 6=4+5
Upto 10000(17units)	47.74(31.65)	14.61(9.69)	3.51(2.32)	65.86(43.67)	84.97(56.33)	150.83(100.0)
10000-15000(140units)	455.77(42.55)	79.77(7.45)	21.44(2.0)	556.98(52.0)	514.25(48.0)	1071.23(100.0)
15000-20000(99 units)	190.61(41.46)	58.78(12.78)	12.28(2.67)	261.67(56.91)	198.11(43.09)	459.78(100.0)
Above 20000(74 units)	144.49(40.37)	37.13(10.37)	6.26(1.75)	187.88(52.49)	170.02(47.50)	357.90(100.0)
Total (330 units)	838.61(41.11)	190.29(9.33)	43.49(2.13)	1072.39(52.57)	967.35(47.43)	2039.74(100.0)
Correlation Coefficient (r)= 0.99						

Note: Figures in the parentheses indicate percentages to total
Source: Field survey

Aggregate Pattern in Total Sample Group

The aggregate pattern of funds mobilization for the construction of houses on the basis of monthly income of the total sample groups are shown in Table 16.

It is clear that out of the total funds required for the construction of houses in all the income categories, the share of informal sources of funds is more than the formal sources. About 52.27 per cent of funds are from informal and 47.43 per cent of funds are secured from formal sources. In informal sources, it is said that the shares of funds from personal savings are relatively higher with 41.11 per cent to that of 9.33 per cent of funds from money lenders and 2.13 per cent from other sources. About 52.27 per cent of funds are from informal and 47.43 per cent of funds are secured from formal sources. Within the different monthly income groups, select banks extended loans to number of housing units in the income range of Rs.10000-15000 of sample borrowers.

In informal sources, it is that the shares of funds from personal savings are relatively higher with 41.11 per cent to that of 9.33 per cent of funds from money lenders and 2.13 per cent from other sources. Thus, it is clear that funds from personal savings play a key role in the construction of houses in all income categories. The coefficient of correlation (r) between total informal sources and formal sources is 0.99. Hence, it may be concluded that two variables i.e., informal sources and formal funds for housing finance are positively correlated.

CHAPTER–6

PROBLEMS OF BORROWERS AND COMMERCIAL BANKS.

INTRODUCTION

The present Chapter deals with various problems faced by both the sample borrowers in availing loans from the banks and the sample banks in sanctioning and recovering the loans from the borrowers. Besides, the satisfaction levels of sample borrowers and their opinions to overcome the problems faced by them are also highlighted. The relevant data and information have been collected through interviews, personal observations and the schedules.

PROBLEMS OF SAMPLE BORROWERS

Sample borrowers of residential house builders are facing number of problems. The problems of the sample borrowers include preparation of documents, delay of sanction, surety and security, rules and regulations, incidental expenses, insufficient loan amount, insurance cost and pre-payment burden.

Bank-wise Problems of Sample Borrowers

Problems of the sample borrowers while borrowing the loans from the banks are embodied in the Table 6.1. Out of 330 sample borrowers, 175 have been facing different kinds of problems. It may be said that the magnitude of the problem is slightly pronounced in AB when compared to other select banks. About 64.15 per cent of the sample borrowers opined that they have problems in dealing with the bank. Very least per cent i.e., 30.0 per cent borrowers said that they faced problems in IB. It indicates that the IB is providing more facilities as customer friendly with other banks.

The intensity of the problems varied from bank to bank. The problem of surity and security is more in SBI. About 48.0 per cent of borrowers from SBI expressed that they would experience difficulty in providing surity and security. With regard to AB, the problem of rules and regulations is having more intensity, which records highest of 59.43 per cent, when compared to all problems related to sample banks. In case of SB, rules and regulations and insurance have the same intensity with 51.85 per cent each. In IB also, there are two problems such as rules and regulations and surity and security representing 30.0 per cent of its sample. Out of the total number of borrowers, 48.79 per cent of borrowers are suffering with the problem of rules and regulations, 46.67 per cent with surity and security, 42.42 per cent with incidental expenses, 29.70 per cent with insurance cost, 25.45 per cent with insufficient sanction of loan amount; 21.52 per cent with of delay in processing of loan application, 19.09 per cent of sample borrowers with preparation of documentation and 6.36 per cent with pre-payment problem. Of all the sample borrowers, the sample borrowers of SB face more problems as of 29 sample borrowers face on an average of 4.97 number of problems and the least is recorded with AB with its 68 sample borrowers, on an average face 4.10 number of problems. Thus, it is observed that the problem of rules and regulations is more in all the select banks.

Hypothesis Formulated and Tested

It is presumed that '*there are no significant differences between select public sector banks and problems of sample borrowers*'.

The calculated value of Chi-Square Value (X^2) is 11.6. The critical value at 5 per cent level of significance for 3 degrees of freedom is 7.815. The calculated value is more than the Table value. Thus, a null hypothesis is rejected.

Table 1
Problems of Sample Borrowers in Select Commercial Banks

Sample Bank	Total No. of Borrowers	No. of Total Borrowers not Facing Problems	No.of Total Borrowers facing Problems	Number of borrowers facing the problems of: Prepa-ration of Docu-ments	Delay in Processing of Loan Application	Surity / Security	Rules & Regulations	Incidental Expenses	In-sufficient Loan	Insurance	Pre Payment	Average No. of Problems per Borrowers*
SBI	150(100.0)	78(52.0)	72(48.0)	22(14.67)	31(20.67)	72(48.0)	64(42.67)	68(45.33)	39(26.0)	34(22.67)	10(6.67)	4.72
AB	106(100.0)	38(35.85)	68(64.15)	27(25.47)	28(26.42)	54(50.94)	63(59.43)	43(40.57)	26(24.53)	32(30.19)	06(5.66)	4.10
SB	54(100.0)	25(46.30)	29(53.70)	12(22.22)	09(16.67)	22(40.74)	28(51.85)	25(46.30)	16(29.63)	28(51.85)	04(7.41)	4.97
IB	20(100.0)	14(70.0)	06(30.0)	02(10.0)	03(15.0)	06(30.0)	06(30.0)	04(20.0)	03(15.0)	04(20.0)	01(5.0)	4.83
Total	330(100.0)	155(46.97)	175(53.03)	63(19.09)	71(21.52)	154(46.67)	161(48.79)	140(42.42)	84(25.45)	98(29.70)	21(6.36)	4.53

Chi – Square Value X^2 - calculated value 11.6
Level of Significance (%) - 5
degrees of Freedom - 3
Critical Value of Chi-Square - 7.815

Note: Figures in the parentheses indicate percentage to total
* Multiple responses
Source: field survey

Income-wise Distribution of Sample Borrowers Facing Problems

The intensity of problems varies from borrower to borrower in relation to their income level as shown in Table 2. Total sample borrowers are divided into four categories based on their monthly income viz., upto Rs.10000; Rs.10000-Rs.15000; Rs.15000-Rs.20000; and more than Rs.20000. Borrowers in the lowest income group having upto Rs.10000 income are 15, but only 4 of them accounting for 26.67 per cent in the group faced the problems with sample banks. About 40.71 per cent and 89.90 per cent of the borrowers are experiencing the problems with select banks in income group of second and third categories respectively. But, sample borrowers with more than Rs.20000 monthly income are 25 forming 33.78 per cent of the total sample group. They are also experienced the problems in taking the loan from sample banks. Almost all income groups of sample borrowers are experiencing the problems equally.

Hypothesis Formulated and Tested

It is presumed that *'there are no significant differences between income level and problems of sample borrowers'*.

The calculated value of Chi-Square Value (X^2) 75.93 is greater than the critical value at 5 per cent level of significance for 3 degrees of freedom is 7.815. Hence, a null hypothesis is rejected.

Problem of Documentation

Documentation is an important factor at the time of applying for house loan in sample banks. The applicants have to submit the loan application along with required documents to select banks. The details of documents to be submitted for housing finance are listed as under:

- Duly filled in application;
- Proof of employment and salary certificate for self and spouse (if employed) / Balance sheet for last 3 years in the case of professionals, businessmen and self employed persons;

Table 2
Income-Wise Distribution of Sample Borrowers Facing Problems

Monthly Income (Rs.)	*Total No. of Borrowers*	*No. of Total Borrowers not Facing the Problems*	*No.of Total Borrowers facing Problems*	*Number of borrowers facing the problems of*								*Average No. of Problems per Borrowers**
				Preparation of Documents	*Delay in Processing of Loan Application*	*Surity / Security*	*Rules & Regulations*	*Incidental Expenses*	*Insufficient Loan*	*Insurance*	*Pre Payment*	
Upto 10000	17(5.15)	13(76.47)	04(23.53)	-	01(6.67)	03(20.0)	03(20.0)	02(13.33)	-	02(13.3 3)	-	4.12
10000-15000	140(42.42)	83(59.29)	57(40.71)	19(13.38)	23(16.20)	52(37.14)	48(33.80)	42(29.58)	21(14.79)	22(15.49)	02(1.43)	4.04
15000-20000	99(30.00)	10(10.10)	89(89.90)	33(33.33)	38(38.38)	78(78.79)	87(87.88)	77(77.78)	54(54.55)	64(64.65)	10(10.10)	4.95
Above 20000	74(22.42)	49(66.22)	25(33.78)	11(15.07)	9(12.33)	21(28.76)	23(31.50)	19(26.03)	9(12.33)	10(13.70)	9(12.16)	4.50
Total	330(100.0)155(46.97)	175(53.03)	63(19.09)	71(21.52)	154(46.67)	161(48.79)	140(42.42)	84(25.45)	98(29.70)	21(6.36)	4.53	

Chi - Square Value X^2 - calculated value 75.93
Level of Significance (%) - 5
Degrees of Freedom - 3
Critical Value of Chi-Square - 7.815

Note: Figures in the parentheses indicate percentage to total
* Multiple responses
Source: Field survey

- Income Tax/Wealth Tax returns for the past 3 years;
- Proof of other sources of income like rent, interest on investment, if any;
- Copy of Agreement of Sale/Sale Deed of the property;
- Demand Draft/Chalan towards payment of (1) processing fees (2) legal charges and (3) administration;
- Duly filled in guarantor forms;
- Estimated of the proposed construction certified by the qualified engineer/authorities;
- No objection certificate from the revenue authorities;
- LIC policy certificate on hand;
- NIL Encumbrances Certificate for 13 years;
- Approved building plan;
- Parent documents for 30 years;
- Title deed;
- Inspection report from qualified civil engineer/ architect;

All sample banks insist on similar type of documents. Out of 330 sample borrowers from all sample banks, 63 sample borrowers feel difficulty in the preparation of document for sanction of the housing loans. Out of 63 sample borrowers experienced the problem in preparation of loan documentation, while the highest of 27 sample borrowers (25.47 per cent) in recorded in AB, the lowest of 2 borrowers (10.0 per cent) in IB. Next to AB, 22 borrowers of SBI and 12 loanees of SB could feel the problem concerning the preparation of loan documentation (see Table 1).

Delay in Sanction of Loans

Owing to delay in the sanction of loans, the select borrowers experienced the problems. In general, select banks after taking borrowers loan applications they will sanction the loans in different time lags. Data with regard to these lags involved in select banks are portrayed in Table 3.

Table 3
Distribution of Sample Borrowers According to Time Involvement in the Sanction of House Loan

Time taken in Sanctioning Loans (in days)	No. of Borrowers				
	SBI	*AB*	*SB*	*IB*	*Total*
Upto 15	38(25.33)	29(27.36)	19(35.18)	06(30.0)	92(27.88)
15-30	45(30.0)	37(34.91)	26(48.15)	09(45.0)	117(35.45)
30-45	33(22.0)	09(8.49)	06(11.11)	-	48(14.55)
45-60	26(17.33)	25(23.58)	03(5.56)	03(15.0)	57(17.27)
Above 60	08(5.33)	06(5.66)	-	02(10.0)	16(4.85)
Total	150(100.0)	106(100.0)	54(100.0)	20(100.0)	330(100.0)

Note: Figures in the parentheses indicate percentages to the total
Source: Field Survey

It is evident that about 35.45 per cent of total sample borrowers are sanctioned loans in 15–30 days; 27.88 per cent of in 15 days; 17.27 per cent in 45-60 days; 14.55 per cent in 30-45 days; and 4.85 per cent after 60 days of application date. There is wide variation of delay in sanctioning loans among the banks under study. About 10.0 per cent of the sample borrowers in IB are receiving loans in more than 60 days. The maximum number of sample borrowers have taken loans for housing construction in 15-30 days in all the select banks. Further, it is significant to note that with in the sample banks, SB sanctions loans more quickly. As large as 35.18 per cent of its borrowers are sanctioned loans within 15 days while none of its customers got loans after 60 days.

Problem of Surity and Security

Another great hurdle that the sample borrowers faced at the times of receiving the loans from select banks is adhering to surity and security conditions.

For analysis, surity and security is classified into three aspects namely, (i) Title of the property (ii) Guarantee and (iii) Collateral security.

Table 4 focuses on the problems regarding surity and security in the select commercial banks. It is clear that out of 330 sample borrowers from all select banks, 154 (46.67 per cent) experienced the problem and 176 not faced the problem of surety and security. Among all the select banks, the problem of surety and security is high in SBI, followed by AB, SB and IB. In all the select banks, problem of guarantee is more pronounced with 23.94 per cent when compared to other surity problems such as title of the property and collateral security. Problem of guarantee is also more in AB when compared to other banks. The reason is that banks demand their customers to arrange guarantee for 5 to 20 years.

Table 4
Distribution Of Sample Borrowers Facing Surity And Security Problem

	No. of Borrowers				
Problem of Borrower	*SBI*	*AB*	*SB*	*IB*	*Total*
Title of the property	28(18.67)	19(17.92)	08(14.81)	02(10.0)	57(17.27)
Guarantee	36(24.0)	29(27.36)	11(20.37)	03(15.0)	79(23.94)
Collateral security	08(5.33)	06(5.66)	03(5.56)	01(5.0)	18(5.46)
Total 1+ 2+ 3	72(48.0)	54(50.94)	22(40.74)	06(30.0)	154(46.67)
Borrowers not facing the problem	78(52.0)	52(49.06)	32(59.26)	14(70.0)	176(53.33)
Total sample 4+ 5	150(100.0)	106(100.0)	54(100.0)	20(100.0)	330(100.0)

Chi – Square Value X^2 - 3.88
Level of Significance (%) - 5
Degrees of Freedom - 3
Critical Value of Chi-Square - 7.815

Note:
1. Figures in the parentheses indicate percentages to the total
2. X^2 calculated for the problems regarding surety and security and problems faced by the sample borrowers in select commercial banks.

Source: Field Survey

It is becoming hurdle on the part of the customers to arrange that much of guarantee to get the house loan. It is observed that some of the sample borrowers faced the problem to submit their joint property title as securities.

Hypothesis Formulated and Tested

It is presumed that *'there are no significant differences between the problems of borrowers regarding surity and security in select commercial banks'*.

It is evident that the calculated value of Chi-square is 3.88 and the critical value is 7.815 at 5 per cent level of significance for 3 degrees of freedom. The calculated value is less than the Table value. Hence, the null hypothesis is accepted.

Rules and Regulations

Usually banks follow some rules and regulations to grant housing finance. These rules and regulations do not help to finance the total cost of the plot, repayment schedules, plinth area criteria, not considering the future/other income and built area criteria.

Table 5 contains the data relating to the problems faced by the sample borrowers regarding the rules and regulations of sample banks.

Table 5
Distribution of Sample Borrowers Facing the Problems of Rules and Regulations

Problem of Borrower	*No. of Borrowers*				
	SBI	*AB*	*SB*	*IB*	*Total*
Total cost of plot not financed	24(16.0)	23(21.70)	11(20.37)	04(20.0)	62(18.79)
Repayment Schedule	12(8.0)	10(9.43)	08(14.81)	01(5.0)	31(9.39)
Non-consideration future income	10(6.67)	08(7.55)	04(7.41)	01(5.0)	23(6.97)
Plinth area criteria	12(8.0)	12(11.32)	03(5.56)	-	27(8.18)
Built area criteria	06(4.0)	10(9.43)	02(3.70)	-	18(5.45)
Total 1+2+3+4+5	64(42.67)	63(59.43)	28(51.85)	06(30.0)	161(48.79)
Borrowing not facing the problem	86(57.33)	43(40.57)	26(48.15)	14(70.0)	169(51.21)
Total sample 4+5	150(100.0)	106(100.0)	54(100.0)	20(100.0)	330(100.0)

Chi – Square Value X^2 - 10.08
Level of Significance (%) - 5
Degrees of Freedom - 3
Critical Value of Chi-Square - 7.815

Note:
1. Figures in the parentheses indicate percentages to the total.
2. X^2 calculated for the problems regarding rules and regulations and problems faced by the sample borrowers in select commercial banks

Source: Field Survey

It is evident that among 330 sample borrowers, 51.21 per cent of borrowers in all the select banks do not suffer with the problem of rules and regulations. Out of 161 borrowers, who encountered with this problem in all the sample banks, 64 borrowers are from SBI and 63 borrowers from AB. It means that the intensity of this problem is more or less equal among the borrowers of SBI and AB. Very less number of borrowers of IB experienced with this problem. Out of all the rules and regulations, such as total cost of plot not financed, repayment schedule, non-consideration of future/other income, plinth and built areas, the problem of total cost of plot not financed was the major one when compared to other followed by plinth and built areas and repayment schedule. This is because, the banks do not extend loan facility for purchase of plot. Banks believe that recovery of loan would be prefect from the borrowers those who could acquire plot on their own. Banks fix the repayment schedule by considering the monthly income, period of service and family size. But, due to some unexpected and unforeseen expenditure in some months, borrowers failed to move according to the fixed repayment schedule.

Hypothesis Formulated and Tested

It is proposed that '*there are no significant differences between problems regarding rules and regulations faced by the sample borrowers in select commercial banks*'.

The calculated value of Chi–Square Value (X^2) is 10.08 and the Table value is 7.815 at 5 per cent level of significance for 3 degrees of freedom. The calculated value is much greater than Table value. Thus, the null hypothesis is rejected.

Incidental Expenses

At the time of sanctioning the loan, sample borrowers have to pay a fixed per cent of amount to sample banks for official expenses. They are processing expenses, legal expenses, and registration charges, stamp duty, administration expenses and the like. But along with above expenses, selected sample borrowers will agree to pay some incidental expenses also. They have to pay unofficial expenses like expenses to visit the relevant offices frequently. These expenses are also different from of one borrower to another borrower. In general, the select public sector banks take a fixed percentage of amounts from the selected sample borrowers as registration fees, processing fees, administration fees, legal expenses and stamp duty. All these expenses are officially taken from the sample borrowers.

Table 6
Distribution of Sample Borrowers Facing the Problem of Incidental Expenses

Incidental Expenses (in percentage over sanctioned of loan)	*No. of Borrowers*				
	SBI	*AB*	*SB*	*IB*	*Total*
Upto 1	32(21.33)	28(26.42)	16(29.63)	03(15.0)	79(23.94)
1-2	26(17.33)	08(7.55)	07(12.96)	01(5.0)	42(12.73)
Above 2	10(6.67)	07(6.60)	02(3.70)	-	19(5.76)
Total (1+2+3)	68(45.33)	43(40.57)	25(46.30)	04(20.0)	140(42.42)
Borrowers not facing the problem	82(54.67)	63(59.43)	29(53.70)	16(80.0)	190(57.58)
Total sample 4+5	150(100.0)	106(100.0)	54(100.0)	20(100.0)	330(100.0)

Chi – Square Value X^2 - 5.74
Level of Significance (%) - 5
Degrees of Freedom - 3
Critical Value of Chi-Square - 7.815

Note:
1. Figures in the parentheses indicate percentages to the total
2. X^2 calculated for the problems regarding incidental expenses and problems faced by the sample borrowers in select commercial banks

Source: Field survey

Table 6 depicts the number of sample borrowers have been faced by problems of incidental expenses from select banks in constructing houses. It is clear that out of 330 sample borrowers of select banks, 42.42 per cent of borrowers have faced the problem of incidental expenses. Among all the select banks, 79 borrowers paid incidental expenses upto 1 per cent of their loan sanctioned, 42 borrowers paid 1-2 per cent of the loan and 19 borrowers paid above 2 per cent of the loan sanctioned. The third category borrowers paid it for loan approval. Among all the select banks, the problem of incidental expenses is more in SBI, followed by AB, SB and IB.

Hypothesis Formulated and Tested

It is hypothesized that '*there are no significant differences between problems faced by the sample borrowers with regarding to incidental expenses and select public sector commercial banks*'.

The calculated value of Chi-Square (X^2) is 5.74 and Table value at 5 per cent level of significance for 3 degrees of freedom is 7.815. The calculated value is less than the Table value. Thus, a null hypothesis is accepted.

Insufficient Loan Amount

Insufficient loan amount is another problem being faced by the sample borrowers from the banks. This problem is different from borrower to borrower and from bank to bank. Table 7 shows the details of the distribution of sample borrowers facing the problem of insufficient loan amount. It is evident that out of the total sample borrowers of all select commercial banks only 25.45 per cent of borrowers faced this problem. About 50 per cent of borrowers who suffered with insufficient loan amount are mainly due to the reason of 'future and other income not considering', followed by low estimated cost and plinth and built areas. But in case of AB, the reason of plinth and built areas are not appeared. Among all the select commercial banks, more number of borrowers from SBI has suffered with insufficient loan amount due to all the three

Table 7
Distribution of Sample Borrowers Facing the Problem of Insufficient Loan Amount

	No. of Borrowers				
Reasons	*SBI*	*AB*	*SB*	*IB*	*Total*
Below Estimated cost	11(7.33)	09(8.49)	04(7.41)	01(5.0)	25(7.58)
Future and other income not considering	18(12.00)	12(11.32)	08(14.81)	02(10.0)	40(12.12)
Plinth area criteria	10(6.67)	05(4.72)	04(7.41)	-	19(5.76)
Total 1+2+3	39(26.00)	26(24.53)	16(29.63)	03(15.0)	84(25.45)
Borrowing not facing the problem	111(74.00)	80(75.47)	38(70.37)	17(85.0)	246(74.55)
Total sample 4+5	150(100.0)	106(100.0)	54(100.0)	20(100.0)	330(100.0)

Chi – Square Value X^2 - 6.09
Level of Significance (%) - 5
Degrees of Freedom - 3
Critical Value of Chi-Square - 7.815

Note:
1. Figures in the parentheses indicate percentages to the total
2. X^2 calculated for the problems regarding insufficient loan amount and problems faced by the sample borrowers in select commercial banks

Source: Field survey

reasons when compared to other banks. The problem of insufficient loan amount is less with IB. Because, the borrowers of IB have not applied loan for huge amounts and so the bank sanctioned the applied amount. It is inferred that the banks consider only present income and paying capacity of the households.

Hypothesis Formulated and Tested

It is presumed that *'there are no significant differences between problems of insufficient loan amount in select commercial banks'*.

The calculated value of Chi-Square *(X^2)* is (6.09) less than the Table value (7.815) at 5 per cent level of significance for 3 degrees of freedom. Thus, the null hypothesis is accepted.

Insurance Cost

Insurance cost is another problem faced by the sample borrowers. The select public sector commercial banks generally cutoff a fixed amount from the sanctioned loan towards insurance cover/cost. Table 8 indicates the distribution of sample borrowers facing the problem of insurance cost.

Table 8
Distribution of Sample Borrowers Facing the Problem of Insurance Cost

	No. of Borrowers				
Reasons	*SBI*	*AB*	*SB*	*IB*	*Total*
Loan cover	28(18.67)	26(24.53)	16(29.63)	03(15.0)	73(22.12)
Term assurance	06(4.0)	06(5.66)	12(22.22)	01(5.0)	25(7.58)
Total 1+2	34(22.67)	32(30.19)	28(51.85)	04(20.0)	98(29.70)
Borrowing not facing the problem	116(77.33)	74(69.81)	26(48.15)	16(80.0)	232(70.30)
Total sample 3+4	150(100.0)	106(100.0)	54(100.0)	20(100.0)	330(100.0)

Chi – Square Value X^2 - 17.21
Level of Significance (%) - 5
Degrees of Freedom - 3
Critical Value of Chi-Square - 7.815

Note :
1. Figures in the parentheses indicate percentages to the total
2. X^2 calculated for the problems regarding insurance cover and problems faced by the sample borrowers in select commercial banks

Source: Field survey

It is clear that out of 98 borrowers from all select commercial banks, highest of 34 borrowers encountered the problem of 'insurance cost'. This problem is very less with IB. Only 4 borrowers out of 20 have suffered with this problem. Most of the borrowers from all the select commercial banks under study experienced that loan cover is the major problem than the term assurance. Borrowers of SBI, AB and SB have experienced with the problem of insurance cost more or less equal.

Hypothesis Formulated and Tested

It is hypothesised that '*there are no significant differences between problems of insurance cover/cost in select commercial banks*'. .

The calculated value of Chi-Square (X^2) is 17.21 and the Table value 7.815 at 5 per cent level of significance for 3 degrees of freedom. The calculated value is more than the Table value. Thus, the null hypothesis is rejected.

Pre-Payment

Another problem of the sample borrowers is pre-payment.

It is obvious that some borrowers are willing to pay the installment amount before the repayment period. In this connection, instead of reducing the interest for early repayment, select commercial banks are taking 2.0 per cent of penal interest from the outstanding balance. The problem of pre-payment of loan is presented in Table 9.

Table 9
Distribution of Sample Borrowers Facing the Problem of Pre - Payment

Name of the Bank	*Total Borrowers*	*Total No. of Borrowers Faced the Problem*	*Total No. of Borrowers Not Faced the Problem*
SBI	150(100.0)	10(6.67)	140(93.33)
AB	106(100.0)	06(5.66)	100(94.34)
SB	54(100.0)	04(7.41)	50(92.59)
IB	20(100.0)	01(5.0)	19(95.0)
Total	330(100.0)	21(6.36)	309(93.64)

Note: Figures in the parentheses indicate percentages to the total
Source: Field survey

It is evident that out of 330 sample borrowers, only 6.36 per cent of borrowers faced the problem of pre-payment of loan. The problem is more with SBI followed by AB, SB and IB. In IB, very least number i.e., only one borrower experienced this problem. More number of borrowers cleared the loan in advance in SB when compared to other commercial banks.

Difference Between Estimated Cost and Total Actual Cost in House Construction

As per the rules and regulation of sample banks, the estimated cost of proposed house will be taken into consideration for sanction of far-limits. Difference between estimated cost and total actual cost is one of the problems of house builders. The sample borrower has to submit the estimated cost plan, which is attested by the builder and the civil engineer or architect to the bank. Table 10 to 13 gives the details of estimated and actual costs and the difference between these two in respect of sample respondents.

Difference between Estimated and Actual Cost of Construction of Housing Units Financed by State Bank of India

Table 10 gives the comparison of estimated cost and total actual cost of housing units financed by SBI.

Table 10
Comparison of Estimated and Actual Costs of Housing Units Financed by SBI

(Rs. in lakhs)

Category of Estimated Cost	*No. of Housing Units*	*Estimated Cost*	*Actual Cost*	*% age of Excess of Actual Cost and Estimated Cost*
Up to 2	28(18.67)	39.93	52.24	30.83
2-4	40(26.67)	114.23	159.87	39.95
4-6	43(28.67)	205.97	320.96	55.83
6-8	27(18.0)	188.02	280.0	48.92
Above 8	12(11.32)	130.34	182.23	39.81
Total	150(100.0)	678.49	995.30	46.69

Note: Figures in the parentheses indicate percentages to total
Source: Field survey

For purpose of analysis, the sample borrowers are classified into 5 categories on the basis of estimated cost. The total estimated cost exceeded to that of total actual cost by 46.69 per cent in respect of 150 housing units financed by SBI. The difference is the highest at 55.83 per cent in Rs.4-6 lakhs estimated category. The lowest difference at 30.83 per cent is upto Rs.2 lakhs category. In other categories it has varied between 39.65 per cent and 48.92 per cent. Thus, aggregate actual cost exceeds considerably high over the estimated cost.

Difference Between Estimated and Actual Cost of Construction of Housing Units Financed by Andhra Bank

Table 11 depicts the details of estimated cost and actual cost of sample housing units financed by AB.

Table 11
Comparison of Estimated and Actual Costs of Housing Units Financed by AB

Category of Estimated Cost	*No. of Housing Units*	*Estimated Cost*	*Actual Cost*	*% age of Excess of Actual Cost and Estimated Cost*
Up to 2	16(15.09)	29.28	46.32	58.20
2-4	41(38.68)	143.56	182.67	27.24
4-6	25(23.58)	136.75	196.27	43.52
6-8	19(17.92)	125.26	153.68	22.69
Above 8	05(4.72)	45.27	52.36	15.66
Total	106(100.0)	480.12	631.30	31.49

Note: Figures in the parentheses indicate percentages to total
Source: Field survey

It is observed that the actual cost of 106 housing units financed by AB has exceeded by 31.49 per cent over the estimated cost. Of the five categories, the lowest category has reported the maximum variation between estimated and actual cost at 58.20 per cent followed by next category of Rs.4-6 lakhs range with 43.52 per cent, Rs.2-4 lakhs range with 27.24 per cent, Rs.6-8 lakhs range with 22.69 per cent and the lowest variation being in above Rs.8 lakhs range with 15.66 per cent.

Difference Between Estimated and Actual Cost of Construction of Housing Units Financed by Syndicate Bank

Table 12 provides a comparative picture of estimated and actual cost of housing units assisted by SB.

Table 12

Comparison of Estimated and Actual Costs of Housing Units Financed by SB

(Rs. in lakhs)

Category of Estimated Cost	*No. of Housing Units*	*Estimated Cost*	*Actual Cost*	*% age of Excess of Actual Cost and Estimated Cost*
Up to 2	09(16.67)	15.00	21.54	43.60
2-4	26(48.15)	91.26	122.73	34.48
4-6	12(22.22)	71.94	89.28	24.10
6-8	05(9.26)	38.27	52.63	37.52
Above 8	02(3.70)	18.67	22.23	19.07
Total	54(100.0)	235.14	308.41	31.16

Note: Figures in the parentheses indicate percentages to total
Source: Field survey

In aggregate, the actual cost of construction of 54 housing units has surpassed by 31.16 per cent over the estimated cost. Similar trend of actual cost exceeding estimates is prevailed in all the five categories of housing units. However there is some difference in degrees of variation between these two costs. High difference is found at 43.60 per cent in the category of upto Rs2 lakhs housing units and the low contrast at 19.07 per cent is found in Rs.4-6 lakhs category. In other three categories, the variation ranges between 37.52 per cent and 24.10 per cent. It can be deduced from the analysis that the actual cost of construction generally exceeds estimated cost of housing units.

Difference between Estimated and Actual Cost of Construction of Housing Units Financed by Indian Bank

Table 13 contains the comparative figures of estimated and total actual cost of housing units financed by IB.

Table 13
Comparison of Estimated and Actual Costs of Housing Units Financed by IB

(Rs. in lakhs)

Category of Estimated Cost	*No. of Housing Units*	*Estimated Cost*	*Actual Cost*	*Percentage of Excess of Actual Cost and Estimated Cost*
Up to 2	03(15.0)	3.50	4.68	33.71
2-4	13(65.0)	52.02	67.26	29.30
4-6	04(20.0)	26.28	32.79	24.77
6-8	-	-	-	-
Above 8	-	-	-	-
Total	20(100.0)	81.80	104.73	28.03

Note: Figures in the parentheses indicate percentages to total
Source: Field survey

Of the total 20 sample housing units financed by IB, three belong to the estimated cost group upto Rs.2 lakhs range and the remaining belong to Rs.2-4 lakhs and Rs.4-6 lakhs. The total actual cost of all these housing units has exceeded by 28.03 per cent over the estimated cost. And within the three classified categories, actual cost has exceeded the estimated cost by 33.71 per cent in the lower category, 29.30 per cent and 24.77 per cent in other categories. Thus, it can be noticed that like in other sample groups, in IB sample group also, the actual cost has exceeded the estimated cost. However, the percentage of excess is less in this group when compared to the other three sample groups of SBI, AB and SB.

Difference Between Estimated and Actual Cost of Total Housing Units

It is normal that there exists difference between the estimated cost and the total actual cost. Because, actual cost exceeds estimated cost due to hike in prices, lack of timely supply of materials, increase in the wages of labourers, demand for more material and the like. Table 14 captures the details of variation between the estimated cost over actual cost of total housing units financed by all select commercial banks.

Table 14
Comparison of Estimated and Actual Costs of Total Sample Housing Units

(Rs. in lakhs)

Category of Estimated Cost	*No. of Housing Units*	*Estimated Cost*	*Actual Cost*	*% age of Excess of Actual Cost and Estimated Cost*
Up to 2	56(16.97)	87.71	124.78	42.26
2-4	120(36.36)	401.07	532.53	32.78
4-6	84(25.45)	440.94	639.30	44.99
6-8	51(15.45)	351.55	486.31	38.33
Above 8	19(5.76)	194.28	256.82	32.19
Total	330(100.0)	1475.55	2039.74	38.24

Note: Figures in the parentheses indicate percentages to total
Source: Field survey

Actual cost of the total sample 330 housing units has exceeded the estimated cost by 36.68 per cent. Out of 330 housing units, the variation between estimated and actual cost is 44.99 per cent in the category of Rs.4-6 lakhs followed by 42.46 per cent of variation in 56 housing units under the category of upto Rs.2 lakhs.The excess of actual cost over the estimated cost is 38.33 per cent in Rs.6.8 lakhs range, 32.78 per cent in Rs.2.4 lakhs range and 32.19 per cent in the high cost housing units having estimated cost above Rs.8 lakhs. On the whole, the percentage of excess of actual cost over estimated cost is 38.24. Thus, it is evident from the analysis that the estimations are always lesser than the actual cost of construction of residential houses. In this context, it is pointed out that the variation is lesser in case of high cost houses.

FACTORS DETERMINNG IN CHOOSING THE SELECT COMMERCIAL BANKS

Borrowers are selecting banks because interest rates of the banks are low and are providing loans for long period. Borrowers feel that select banks are better to that of other financial institutions and money lenders. And some more reasons are low interest, insurance cost, nearness of place, reputation of banks, simple procedures, quick sanctions, additional services, cordial treatment of borrowers, friends and relatives recommendations, sufficient loan amount and easy installment. Borrowers are showing interests in securing lakhs of loans from sample banks and the reasons for these are given in the Table 15.

Of the total sample borrowers, 25.76 per cent of sample borrowers expressed that sample banks sanction the loans quickly, 23.33 per cent of the sample borrowers are influenced by the simple procedure. And 14.55 per cent opined that the banks sanction sufficient loan and remaining 8.48 per cent borrowers have chosen banks on friends and relatives recommendation. Remaining reasons include low interest rates, easy installments, reputation of banks, nice treatment of bankers, insurance cost, nearness of place and new services. Thus, it is evident that house loan seekers have different reasons to choose a lending banker.

Bank-wise analysis reveals that of the sample borrowers of IB, 40.0 per cent of borrowers have preferred this bank because of its simple procedures and 20.0 per cent due to sufficient loan amount and 15.0 per cent of borrowers preferred it for quick sanctions, 10.0 per cent did prefer for its low interest rates and remaining 5.0 per cent of the sample borrowers have chosen it for the insurance cost, nice treatment and easy installments. Out of the total sample borrowers of SB, 37.04 per cent of borrowers favoured the bank for simple procedure, followed by 29.63 per cent for quick sanctions, 14.81 per cent for sufficient loan amount and the remaining borrowers liked for lower interest rate, easy installment, the best treatment of borrowers and the reputation of the bank.

It is evident that in AB, about 32.08 per cent of its sample borrowers preferred the bank for quick sanction, 20.75 per cent due to friends and relatives recommendation and 11.32 per cent for simple procedures. The rest of the sample house loanees have chosen for sufficient loan amounts, easy installments, low interest, nearness to place, best treatment and for insurance cost.

Table 15
Significant Factors Determining in Choosing the Select Public Sector Banks

	No of Borrowers				
Factors	*SBI*	*AB*	*SB*	*IB*	*Total*
Low interest	09(6.0)	06(5.66)	04(7.41)	02(10.00)	21(6.36)
Insurance cost	06(4.0)	02(1.89)	-	01(5.0)	09(2.73)
Near of place	03(2.0)	05(4.72)	-	-	08(2.42)
Reputation bank	10(6.67)	05(4.72)	01(1.85)	-	16(4.85)
Simple procedure	37(24.67)	12(11.32)	20(37.04)	08(40.0)	77(23.33)
QuickSanctions	32(21.33)	34(32.08)	16(29.63)	03(15.0)	85(25.76)
Additional services	05(3.33)	-	-	-	05(1.52)
Cordial treatment of borrowers	07(4.67)	04(3.77)	02(3.70)	01(5.0)	14(4.24)
Friends, relatives recommended	06(4.0)	22(20.75)	-	-	28(8.48)
Sufficient loan amount	27(18.0)	09(8.49)	08(14.81)	04(20.0)	48(14.55)
Easy installment	08(5.33)	07(6.60)	03(5.56)	01(5.0)	19(5.76)
Total sample	150(100.0)	106(100.0)	54(100.0)	20(100.0)	330(100.0)

Note: Figures in the parentheses indicate percentages to total
Source: Field survey

About 24.67 per cent and 21.33 per cent of borrowers are influenced by simple procedures and quick sanctions respectively. About 18.0 per cent of house loanees preferred SBI bank for sufficient loan, but only 6.67 per cent for reputation of the bank. Low interest, easy installment, best treatment, friends and relatives recommendation, insurance cost and additional services, nearness of place are the determinants in choosing the bank for other house loanees. Thus, reasons for choosing a lending banker by the sample borrowers differ from bank to bank. Chart 1 represents the significant factors determining in choosing the select public sector banks.

Chart 1: Significant Factors Determining in Choosing the Select Public Sector Banks

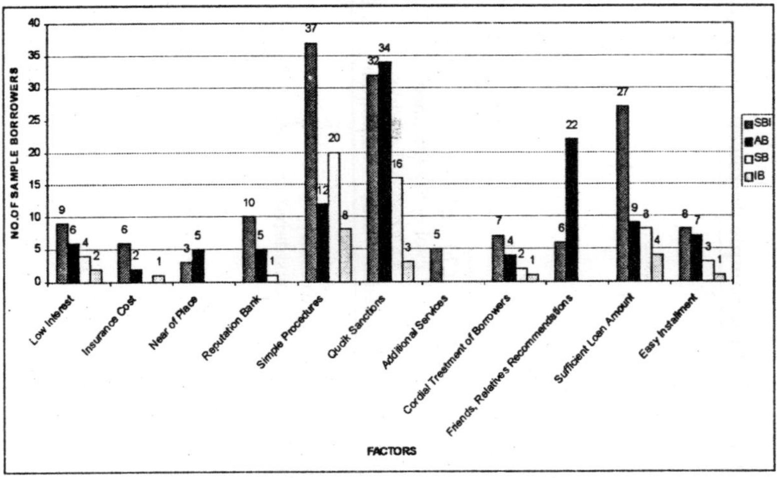

OPINIONS OF THE SAMPLE BORROWER

The sample borrowers have experienced with certain problems at the time of taking loan from select commercial banks. Regarding the problems of the sample borrowers, their opinions were elicited to overcome these problems. The opinions of the sample borrowers are given in the Table 16.

Out of the total 330 sample borrowers, 127 sample borrowers representing 38.48 per cent opined in favour of

Table 16

Opinion of the Sample Borrowers to Overcome the Problems

Opinion of the Borrowers	*Borrowers*				
	SBI	*AB*	*SB*	*IB*	*Total*
The purchase cost of the plot should be financed by sample banks	52(34.67)	48(45.28)	23(42.59)	04(20.0)	127(38.48)
Salary deduction	41(27.33)	12(11.32)	11(20.37)	08(40.0)	72(21.82)
Removing the Insurance facility	32(21.33)	17(16.04)	06(11.11)	01(5.0)	56 (16.97)
Waiving off penalty to prepayment	19(12.67)	20(18.87)	07(12.96)	05(25.0)	51(15.45)
Encourage the non-salaried class	6.00(4.0)	09(8.49)	07(12.96)	02(10.0)	24(7.27)
Total sample	150(100.0)	106(100.0)	54(100.0)	20(100.0)	330(100.0)

Chi–Square Value X^2 - 26.9

Level of Significance (%) - 5

Degrees of Freedom - 12

Critical Value of Chi-Square - 21.026

Note:

1. Figures in the parentheses indicate percentages to total
2. The most significant opinion of the borrower is considered and included in the table.

Source: Field survey

banks providing sufficient loan to purchase house plots, 72 sample borrowers representing 21.82 per cent have expressed that the installment should be stable as far as possible. 56 sample borrowers representing 16.97 per cent viewed that the banks should not change insurance premium at a time. About 51 sample borrowers representing 15.45 per cent opined that banks while 24 sample borrowers representing 7.27 per cent suggested that the encouragement should be made to the non-salaried categories by the select commercial banks should not collect pre-payment charges With in the four select banks, the highest percentage (45.28 per cent) of sample borrowers are from AB who have suggested that the purchase cost of the plot should be financed by sample banks.

In case of deduction of salary as installment also, the highest number of the sample borrowers (40.0 per cent) are from IB. With regard to changing for insurance cost, highest percentage (21.33 per cent) of sample borrowers who opposed it are from SBI. And the highest of 25.0 per cent from IB in case of removing penalty of pre-payment. It may be said that the problems of borrowers of housing loans differ from one commercial bank to other. Opinions of the sample borrowers to overcome the problems is shown Chart 2.

Chart 2: Opinion of the Sample Borrowers to Overcome the Problems

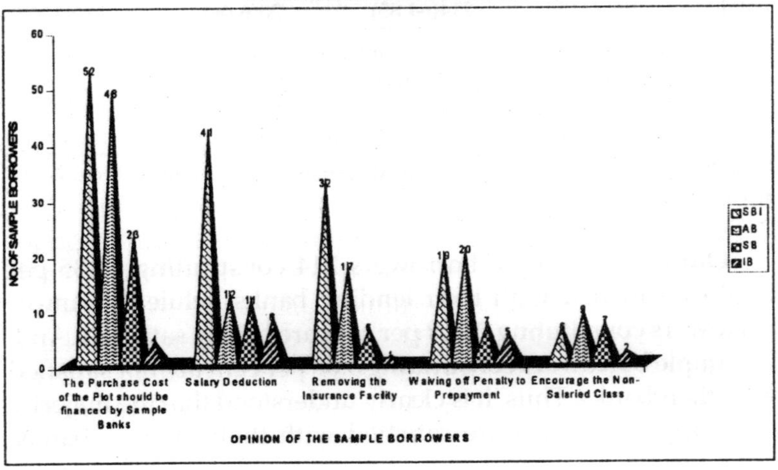

Results of Hypothesis Tested

It is observed that the calculated value of Chi-Square value (X^2) is 26.9 greater than the Table value is 21.026 at 5 per cent level of significance for 12 degrees of freedom. It is concluded that '*there are no significant differences between the opinions/awareness of the sample borrowers of housing loans from public sector commercial banks*' Thus the null hypothesis is rejected.

SATISFACTION LEVEL OF BORROWERS IN RESPECT OF THEIR LENDING BANKS

In a competitive environment, the prospects of any commercial bank depends on customer satisfaction to a large extent. Therefore, it is quite relevant and useful to assess customers satisfaction. Sample borrower's satisfaction levels are shown in the Table 17.

Table 17

Sample Bank	*Satisfaction Level of the Sample Borrowers*			*Total*
	Highly Satisfied	*Satisfied*	*Non-Satisfied*	
SBI	30(20.0)	111(74.0)	09(6.0)	150(100.0)
AB	22(20.75)	77(72.64)	07(6.60)	106(100.0)
SB	32(59.26)	19(35.19)	03(5.55)	54(100.0)
IB	12(60.0)	07(35.0)	01(5.0)	20(100.0)
Total	96(29.09)	214(64.85)	20(6.06)	330(100.0)

Chi – Square Value X^2 - 43.32
Level of Significance (%) - 5
Degrees of Freedom - 6
Critical Value of Chi-Square - 12.592

Note: Figures in the parentheses indicate percentages to total
Source: Field survey

Out of 330 sample borrowers 214 constituting 64.85 per cent are satisfied with their lending banks, while 96 sample borrowers constituting 29.09 per cent are highly satisfied. And, 20 sample borrowers constituting 6.06 per cent are not satisfied with their banks. Thus, it is clearly understood that the majority of sample borrowers are satisfied with their lending banks.

Within the four sample bank groups, the sample borrowers of SBI are more satisfied with 74.0 per cent followed by AB group (72.64 per cent), SB group with (35.19 per cent) and by IB with (35.0 per cent).

It is clear that out of the total 150 sample borrowers of SBI, as many as 111 representing 74.0 per cent expressed that they are satisfied with the services rendered by the bank. About 30 borrowers are highly satisfied while 9 borrowers are satisfied. In AB 77 borrowers constituting 72.64 per cent are satisfied with the customer services rendered by it. Among 54 sample borrowers of SB, 32 borrowers forming 59.26 per cent expressed that they are highly satisfied with the services rendered by the bank. The satisfaction level in IB sample group is almost similar to that of SB. In respect of all the four select public sector banks, more than 95 per cent of their borrowers feel satisfied with their services. It may be conclude that the four select commercial banks have been successful in maintaining goodwill among their borrowers to a large extent. Chart 3 shows the satisfaction level of the sample borrowers.

Chart 3: Satisfaction Level of the Sample Borrowers

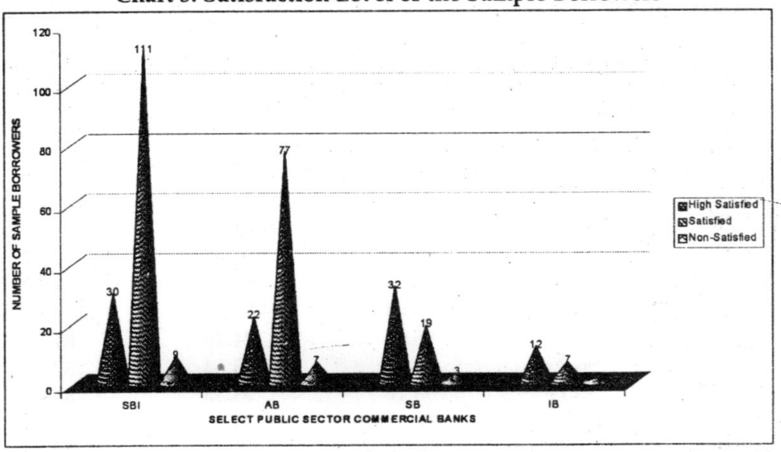

Results of Hypothesis Tested

It is evident that '*there are no significant differences between the satisfaction level of the sample borrowers of housing loans from public sector commercial banks'* as the calculated value of Chi-Square value (X^2) is 43.32. Table value at 5 per cent level of significance for 6 degrees of freedom is 12.592. The calculated value is greater than the Table value. Hence, a null hypothesis is rejected.

PROBLEMS OF THE SELECT COMMERICAL BANKS

Like borrowers, the banks are also facing some problems. Problems of sample Banks, State Bank of India (SBI), Andhra Bank (AB), Syndicate Bank and Indian Bank are analysised separately. Problem is recovery of installments are analyzed in this connection. The analysis is based on the information provided by the managers and officials of these four sample commercial banks.

Rate of Recovery of Loan Installments

The main problem of any select public sector banks is the recovery of installments from its borrowers. The success of any commercial bank is purely depending on its capability of recovering sanctioned loans from the borrowers. Table 19 depicts the details of recovery of loan installments by select banks (Chart 4).

Table 19

Rate of Recovery of Loan Installments in Select Banks

	Recovery Per Cent			
Year	*SBI*	*AB*	*SB*	*IB*
1999-2K	93.26	84.28	86.25	83.41
2000-01	98.02	96.24	92.36	82.71
2001-02	99.0	93.55	86.25	81.62
2002-03	100.0	86.54	95.26	85.0
2003-04	97.36	96.65	94.48	81.98
2004-05	96.25	97.54	95.64	82.37
2005-06	95.11	98.16	98.35	84.30
2006-07	96.43	98.17	98.46	87.56
2007-08	98.35	99.00	98.89	89.90

Calculated 'ANOVA' Value - 25.0395
Level of Significance (%) - 5.000
Degrees of Freedom (n1-1, n2-1) - 3, 24
Critical Value of 'ANOVA' - 4.72

Source: Field survey

Chart 4: Rate of Recovery of Loan Installments in Select Banks

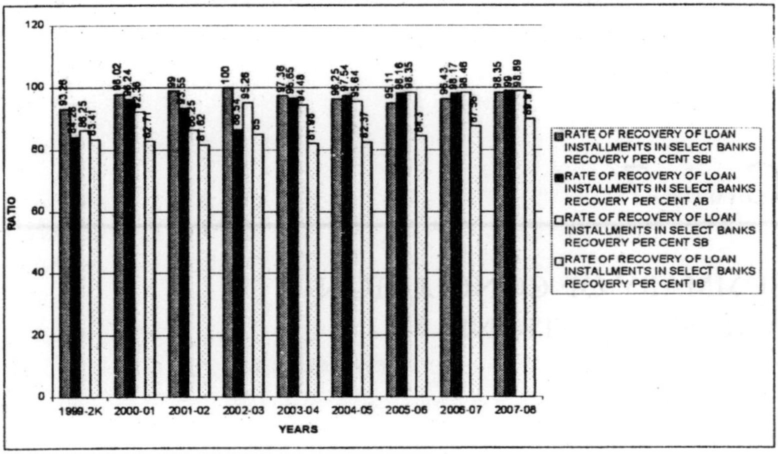

On anlaysis, it is observed that there are fluctuations in the recovery of loan installments in the select public sector banks. SBI has recorded the highest rate of recovery with 100.0 per cent in the year 2002-03 and for the rest of the years its recovery rate varied between 93.0 per cent and 99.0 per cent. In case of AB, the highest recovery rate was 99.00 per cent in 2007-08 and for the rest, recovery rate varied between 84.0 per cent and 98.17 per cent. SB has recovered 98.89 per cent during 2007-08 and in other years its recovery rate range between 86.25 per cent and 98.46 per cent. And, IB has recovered 89.90 per cent in 2007-08 year and between 81.62 per cent and 87.90 per cent in the rest years.

On comparing the rates of recovery of sample commercial banks, it is highest in State Bank of India followed by and Andhra Bank Syndicate Bank. Comparatively, the recovery performance of Indian Bank lags behind the other sample commercial banks.

Results of Hypothesis Tested

The calculated value of 'ANOVA' (25.0395) is greater than the critical value of 'ANOVA' (4.72). Hence the hypothesis, '*there are no significant differences in the select commercial banks in facing the problems regarding recovery of house loans*' is rejected.

CHAPTER–7

SUMMARY OF CONCLUSION AND SUGGESTIONS

INTRODUCTION

Housing is one of the basic needs of every human being. Housing finance is a specialist economic activity of recent origin in India. It is in its infant stage of development and like any other newly emerging system, it also faces certain problems. Commercial banks have been extending financial services for housing activities to individual households and providing term loans at concessional rates of interest to the public housing agencies. The customer of today has also become aware about his needs and requirements of housing finance. The study covers the housing scenario in India, housing finance system in India, design and methodology, profiles and performance of commercial banks, pattern of funds mobilization and the problems encountered by borrowers vis-a-vis banks. The conclusions that emerged from the foregoing analysis are summarized with suitable suggestions for the effective housing finance activity by commercial banks in Kadapa Corporation in particular and in other urban town in general.

CONCLUSIONS

- A better house leads to better standards of living of the people, which in turn makes their life healthy and happy and worth living. Realizing the importance of housing needs in the national economy, institutional arrangements have been made during the recent past to cater to the provision of housing finance in India.

- The relevance of housing as a social need has been felt at different levels viz., national, state and local levels. This reflects in the efforts of the government which has undertaken to improve the housing and habitant conditions by way of financial allocation in the five year plans and in union budgets.
- Before Independence, the housing problem in India had come to the fore and the intensity of the problem had gradually increased thereafter. In 2001, the total population was 1027million. The projected population is 1194 million in 2011and 1417 million in 2021. The share of housing activity in total gross domestic product raised from 3.4 per cent in 2001 to 7.25 per cent in 2005 and to 8.50 per cent by 2006. The shortage of housing stock stood at a staggering figure of 41.0 million in 2001. In qualitative terms, housing conditions such as supply of water, drainage and sanitation are far from satisfactory.
- Under the Indian Constitution, though housing is a state subject, both the Central and State Governments jointly provide assistance for housing. As the Centre has introduced a number of social housing schemes, the state and union territories execute the housing projects with full powers.
- Both in urban and rural areas, the number of households living in one room have shown a declining trend in the last four decades whereas an increasing trend is seen in other larger categories. And the tendency to own a house has shown an increasing trend.
- The Central Government formed an independent ministry for works and housing in 1954 for the development of the housing sector. The Governments have initiated number of schemes and made allocations in the Five Year Plans towards providing housing in the country. In the Eleventh

Five Year Plan, a Working Group was established to estimate the urban housing requirement. The Central Ministry of Rural Development, with an estimated fund of Rs.5401 crores, is planning for 26.53 million additional houses by giving more than 90 per cent priority to the poor, EWS and LIG segments in urban areas.

- Housing finance provides finance at all stages in the development of housing from purchase of plot to the construction of house. It is a specialist economic activity that has gained prominence in recent years. In the past, the housing finance sector was neglected which inturn, created a serious shortage of housing in India. But, there has been a tremendous increase in the competition in the housing finance sector due to the entry of many institutions into the financing market in recent years. And it is envisaged that in the next five years, the housing finance sector will grow at 24.10 per cent.
- As a first step towards the establishment of an institutional structure in the housing finance sector in the country, Housing and Urban Development Corporation (HUDCO) was established in 1970 in public sector. Since its inception, it has been providing loans an integrated, financially viable composition and infrastructure development.
- The Housing Development Finance Corporation (HDFC) was established in 1977 in the private sector and it is the first primary housing institution. The basic objectives of HDFC is to provide finance to individuals, co-operatives and corporate bodies for housing development by channelising household savings as well as funds from capital market into the housing sector. The business model of HDFC is robust and it has been adjudged as a successful housing finance institution both at the national and international level.
- Co-operative housing societies in the country date back to the beginning of the 20th Century. Housing co-operatives have a prominent place since the co-operative movement in the country. The National Co-operative Housing

Federation of India (NCHF) is the national-wide organization of the Indian co-operative housing movement. It was set-up in September 1969 by the apex co-operative housing federation. The basic thrust of its formation was to have an organization at the national level to assume the responsibility of promoting, developing and co-ordinating the activities of housing co-operatives in the country. The NCHF operates 26 apex co-operative housing federations in the states. There are nearly 90000 primary co-operative housing societies with 6.5 million individual members.

- The Insurance Corporations has been participating on a low profile in housing finance till recently. Now, the Life Insurance Corporation Housing Finance limited (LICHFL) is one of the largest housing finance companies in India which has widest marketing net-works. It has more than 2000 branches and 65 areas offices through out the country. It was promoted on 19th June 1989 by LIC and a public issue was made in 1994. LICHFL provides loans to residents and non-residents of India, along with various facilities to their esteemed customers.
- The commercial banking net-work has been the largest mobiliser of household savings in the country. Housing, which was one of the un-touched sectors, has now become an important segment of commercial credit provided both by public and semi-pubic sector banks as well. All commercial banks have been advised by RBI to compute their share of minimum housing allocation at 3 per cent of their incremental deposits. However, the banks are also given the freedom to exceed the limit for housing allocations. Having recognized the potential of the housing finance sector, the commercial banks are stepping forward to participate in the housing finance activity in a big way by establishing specialist housing finance institutions.
- As a sequel to the recommendations of various groups and commissions, National Housing Bank (NHB) was set up exclusively to serve the housing sector on 9th July, 1988 under the National Housing Act 1987, to act and function

as an apex bank. The bank is the primary agent to promote financial and other support to such agencies. Its motto is "Small-man First" and it has been striving towards the goal of "Shelter for All". The main objective is to provide a sound, healthy, viable and cost-effective housing finance system to cater to all segments of the population.

- The performance of NHB in terms of promoting a viable institutional structure in the housing finance sector, mobilization of resources, refinancing activities, recoveries and other duties, as an apex body has been extremely satisfactory.
- In India, the informal sector has played a vital role in extending financial assistance for housing, especially to the poor and low- income households. Informal sector includes money lenders, own sources and borrowings from friends and relatives.
- Commercial banks play a significant role in the Indian economy. They are the heart of Indian financial structure with an ability to add to the supply of money by creating additional purchasing power in the country. By entering into the field of housing finance, the Indian commercial banks play a vital role by providing housing finance. Even in medium urban town like the Kadapa Corporation, a larger number of banks have entered into the field of housing finance to cater to the needs of the customers.
- All the select bank branches reported a rise in key financial variables like deposits, advances and net profit with the exception of SB over the period under reference.
- The liquidity position of the select public sector commercial banks is far from satisfactory.
- The depositors and the lenders of the select commercial banks were not protected. In other words, these banks have not been performing better on the capital adequacy front.
- The equity multiplier of the select commercial banks signifies acquisition of more assets relative to capital base thereby helping to improve the profitability of the banks.

- The financial solvency of the select commercial banks is not satisfactory as interest coverage ratio had never touched the usual norm of 4:1.
- Of the overall net profit margin, AB is comparatively better than that of the remaining three select commercial banks. The performance of IB is much better comparatively with regard to operating efficiency.
- Of all the select public sector banks, AB and IB have enjoyed reasonable return on their respective capital employed throughout the period of study.
- Majority of the borrowers have been constructing houses upto 30 yeas age group. Banks have been giving more preference to the middle-age groups. They give less preference to the borrowers whose age is above 50 years.
- Social status-wise classification of the borrowers reveals that more share of loans is given to other communities (OC) followed by Back-ward caste (BCs) and the least priority to the SCs/STs. In other words, SCs/STs are not given much importance.
- All the select banks have sanctioned loans on the priority of educational background. First priority is given to applicants with higher qualification.
- From the occupational point of view, the banks are showing their interest in sanctioning housing loans especially to the employees, as the repayment is made easy with their fixed source of income. So, the public sector commercial banks have been giving the first priority to the employees, then to the business community and the least priority to the others. The commercial banks have been especially neglecting the borrowers of the non-salaried categories.
- Family size-wise classification reveals that the sample commercial banks have given preference to the borrowers whose family size is 3-5 members and less preference to those family size is above 5 members.
- Monthly income is one of the main aspects being taken into consideration during the time of sanction of loans to

the borrowers. Higher income groups have more importance as compared to lower income groups. As per the opinion of the banks, the recovery of the loans is not upto the mark.

- The pattern of funds mobilization for constructing houses is very essential to any borrower. In this case, most of the problems of the sample borrowers are related to the mobilization of funds.
- The borrowers mobilize funds for the construction of houses through two sources viz., informal sources and formal resources. Personal savings, money lenders and others fall under informal sources and funds from sample public sector banks fall under formal sources. Banks sanction loan upto 85 per cent of the estimated cost of the house/flat.
- Out of the total funds mobilized by the sample borrowers, the informal sources are much greater in share than the formal sources. Of the total informal sources, personal savings apportioned 85 per cent, money lenders 10 per cent and other sources 5 per cent.
- Formal sources concentrate more on sanctioning the loans to the housing units wherein the cost category is between Rs.4 to 6 lakhs. Commercial banks prefer to sanction loans particularly to this category because this category is the middle category of all total categories. From the aggregate point of view also, informal sources have contributed 54.59 per cent of funds whereas formal sources to the tune of 45.41 per cent of funds.
- In AB, informal sources have more or less equally contributed with that of formal sources. But in the case of Rs.4-6 lakhs category, the sanction of formal loans is greater than other categories.
- For the total 54 sample housing units in SB, more loans are provided by formal sources to the Rs.2-4 lakhs cost category when compared to that of other categories. Personal savings have occupied the highest share in

informal sources compared to money lenders and other sources.

- IB has sanctioned housing loans to the borrowers in the range of upto Rs.2 lakhs to Rs.4-6 lakhs categories only. For the total 20 sample units, the total mobilization of funds secured by the sample borrowers in IB is Rs.104.73 lakhs. IB has sanctioned more loans to Rs.2-4 lakhs category than that of other categories.
- Out of 330 sample borrowers, 175 borrowers constituting 53.03 per cent have experienced one problem or the other. And the remaining borrowers constituting 47.27 per cent have not experienced any problems from any select public sector commercial banks.
- Of all the problems faced by the borrowers, the major problem is rules and regulations followed by surety and security and paying the incidental expenses. Other problems such as insufficient loan amount, delay in processing, insurance cost, prepayment and preparation of documents are experienced by lesser number of borrowers.
- With regard to the problem of preparation of documents, most of the sample borrowers have opined that it would be difficult for them to cope up with paper work.
- In the case of period of loan sanctioned, only a few applications took more than 60 days while more applicants were sanctioned within 30 days.
- In respect of surety and security, the problem of arranging guarantee is strongly felt by the sample borrowers followed by title of the property and other security.
- The estimations are always less than the actual cost of construction of residential houses. As compared to all estimated cost categories, there is a lesser difference in the higher cost category.
- In order to overcome the problems and to increase the number of housing units, all sample public sector commercial banks officials opined that they have to finance

the borrowers for purchase of plots also. Most of the borrowers opined that instead of deducting in one go (lum sum). Insurance cost can be collected in installments. Simultaneously, it would be reasonable to cut certain percentage month wise. No penalty for prepayment of loans may not be imposed.

- Majority of the sample borrowers opined that the cost of the plot needs to be considered by commercial banks for financing. Other views expressed by them in order of weightage include introducing salary deduction facility for repayment of house loan installments, removing insurance cost, waiving of prepayment charges and encouraging the non-salaried class groups.
- In respect of all the four select public sector banks, more than 95 per cent of their borrowers feel satisfied with their services. It may be concluded that the select commercial banks have been successful in maintaining goodwill among their borrowers to a large extent.
- The recovery performance is better in SBI as against other sample banks.

RESULTS OF HYPOTHESES TESTED

- The hypothesis that *'there are no significant differences in the credit needs of individuals constructing residential houses'* is accepted.
- The null hypothesis that *'there are no significant differences in the select commercial banks in facing the problems regarding recovery of house loans'* is rejected.
- The null hypothesis that *'there are no significant differences between the opinions/awareness and satisfaction of the sample borrowers of housing loans from public sector commercial banks'* is rejected.

SUGGESTIONS

- The gap between housing supply and demand shall be reduced. In this connection, more institutional agencies for housing finance shall be established. Also new housing schemes shall be introduced by the Government to cater requirements of different segmented groups. Housing loans shall be provided to these segments with low rate of interest.

- It is more important to preserve the existing housing stock before thinking of adding new ones. For this purpose, plans should be envisaged to provide adequate loan facilities for renovation of all such dwelling units.
- Public Sector Commercial Banks shall improve their liquidity condition by strengthening the current assets base further.
- Financial solvency shall be strengthened by enhancing the capital and net worth bases in all the public sector commercial banks.
- The public sector commercial banks should improve the EBIT level so as to cover interest charges. Further, operating expenses shall be controlled in order to improve the operating efficiency of the public sector banks.
- The sample commercial banks have to sanction loans not only to the middle age people but also to the others who are about to get retirement within 10 years also.
- Public sector banks are providing most of their loans to the middle income groups. The tendency of loan syndication should be reduced in middle income groups and they also concentrate on low-income groups. Further, non-salaried people shall also be provided loans by commercial banks.
- Select public sector banks should consider loans to large family of above five members as joint family system still prevails in rural India.
- Public sector banks have to sanction more housing loans to weaker sections of the society like SC, ST and BC communities so as to reduce the imbalances in the society with regard to housing. Empowerment of weaker sections shall be given top priority when the Nation slogan is "Housing for all".

- Public Sector banks should provide finance not only for construction of house but also for purchase of plot so that borrowers need not to depend on money lenders who charge very high rate of interest.
- The commercial banks can sanction upto 95 per cent of the estimated cost of housing units as the actual cost always exceeds estimated cost due to constant inflation of cost of materials and other inputs.
- The commercial banks shall guide the borrowers in the preparation of the estimated cost plans to get quick sanction of housing loans from the banks.
- Public sector banks should reduce time to process the documentation and should try to sanction the loan within 15 to 20 days from the date of application for loan.
- The public sector commercial banks should minimize the processing and administrating charges to improve the clientele.
- Inordinate delays in sanctioning of loans shall be avoided. Even in the case of non-salaried income loanees, the cumbersome procedure prevalent shall be simplified while sanctioning the loans.
- The loan amount shall be estimated based on the latest prices of the inputs to make it more adequate for the purpose of sanctioning loan.
- Processing of verification and documentation should be made simple. Specifically, the number of documents to be submitted for house loan shall be minimized.
- While recovering the loan amount from the beneficiaries, banks should avail the facility of deducting the dues from the salary at source to save time and expenditure of the borrowers and banks.
- Insurance cost should not be deducted in one lumpsum. It should be better if it is added to the monthly installments.
- Pre-settlement of housing loans should be allowed with nominal charges. Further, the borrower should be

encouraged to repay the housing loans ahead of their repayment schedule.

- Competition shall be created among the branches to excel in recovery and best performing branches may be rewarded monetarily. At individual employee level also, performance linked incentives system shall be implemented to motivate employees to step-up monitoring and recovery.
- System for awarding of trophy/ merit certificates shall be introduced for better recovery performance in public sector commercial banks.
- Government should provide guarantee on customer's credit, especially in the case of low income groups.
- Public sector commercial banks shall start more branches in towns to sanction the housing loans. This will help bankers as well as home builders to overcome the problems like delayed sanctions, non-recoveries and the like.
- Bankers shall consider increment of future income of the house seekers while sanctioning the loans.
- Public sector commercial banks are charging penal interest on delayed payments of housing loan installments. It is suggest that at least one/two month's grace period shall be allowed for charging penal interest.
- In order to ensure prompt re-payment by housing loan borrowers, incentives shall be given to all those borrowers who are strictly adhering to the installment schedule.
- Commercial banks can also reduce the interest burden to the borrowers by calculating interest on monthly rest basis. Interest rates on housing loans shall be reduced so as to increase the customer base.
- The Government and NHB can take up necessary steps to make available, reliable and timely information on housing activity.
- The bank employees need to be given proper orientation and training towards development aspects of the commercial banks. They must be proactive in identifying

the specific requirements of the people of their service area and formulate appropriate schemes for enlistment of the standard of living of the people in that region. The staff need to act as change agents to educate the customers and instigate development oriented changes among the urban masses concerning housing sector.

- Banking policies and procedures on housing finance shall be given utmost priority over political influences and interferences in the matters of house loan disbursement and recovery so as to combat the misuse of commercial banks' credit.

SCHEDULES

Housing Finance by Commercial Banks- A Study With Reference to Kadapa Corporation, Andhra Pradesh, Schedule for Borrowers

1. Name of the Respondent :
2. Age :
3. Address :
4. Educational Qualifications *(Put √ mark)*
   a) Matric b) UG
   c) Graduate d) Post Graduate
5. Community *(Put √ mark)*
   a) SC/ST b) BC
   c) Others
6. No. of members in the family :
7. Occupation *(Put √ mark)*
   a) Employee b) Business
   c) Agricultural d) any others
8. Monthly and Yearly Income :
9. Name and Address of the Bank :
10. House hold size :
11. Purpose of Loan *(Put √ mark)*
    a) Purchase of flat/house
    b) Constructions of house
    c) Repairs/Renovation of house
    d) Extension of house

12. Please give the details of Source of funds in your house property?
    a) Personal savings   b) Moneylender
    c) Loan from others
13. Total cost of the house *(Put √ mark)*
    a) upto Rs.200000   b) Rs.200000 - 400000
    c) Rs.400000 - 600000   d) Rs.600000 - 800000
    e) Above Rs. 800000
14. Total estimated cost of the house *(Put √ mark)*
    a) upto Rs.200000   b) Rs.200000 - 400000
    c) Rs.400000 - 600000   d) Rs.600000 - 800000
    e) Above Rs. 800000
15. How much Cost of land?
16. Date of application for loan
    Date......   Month......
    Year......
17. Date of sanction for the house loan :
    Date......   Month......
    Year......
18. Please mention the security details of your house loans b *(Put √ mark)*
    a) Nature of Security offered
    b) Number of Securities provided
    c) Value of Security offered **Rs**
19. Are there any escalation charges due to delay in release of loan? YES / NO
    (If yes please specify) *(Put √ mark)*
    a) Registration fee   b) stamp duty
    c) cost amenities   d) service charges
    e) any other
20. In how many stages the loan was released? *(Put √ mark)*
    a) 3 stages   b) 4 stages
    c) 5 stages   d) 5 stages above

21. What is repayment period of loan?
22. Was the installment amount reasonable? YES/NO
23. In which forms you can select the made of repayment convenient to you?
    a) Deduction of monthly installment
    b) Rules/regulations of the bank
    c) Other (Specify)
24. Are you trying to repay it before? YES/NO
25. If you have received the loan amount after the completion of he construction? YES/NO
26. What is the rate of interest on such loan?
27. What problems did you come across in raising house loan form the bank? *(Put √ mark)*
    a) High rate of interest
    b) Delay in processing loan application
    c) Surety/security problems
    d) Rigid rules and regulation
    e) Insufficient of loan amount
    f) Incidental expenses
    g) Insurance cost
    h) Pre-payment
28. Please specify the reasons for your preference to borrow from the bank *(Put √ mark)*
    a) Low rate of interest
    b) Insurance
    c) Near of place
    d) Reputation bank
    e) Quick sanctions
    f) Additional services
    g) Best treatment of borrowers
    h) Friends and relatives recommended
    i) Simple Procedure
    j) sufficient loan amount

29. Whether insurance is required for home lone? YES / NO

If YES, what type of policy required?

a) Loan cover b) Term assurance

30. If you have received the loan amount after the completion of the construction? YES/NO

31. Was the sanctioned loan released in time by the Bank? YES/ NO

32. Are happy of becoming a loanee of this Bank YES / NO

33. Is any other source better than the Bank loan? YES /NO

34. General

1) Who assisted you in designing the house plan?

2) Do you any problems in getting the approval?YES/NO

35. Are you satisfied with your lending Bank?

a) Highly satisfied b) satisfied

c) not satisfied

Housing Finance by Commercial Banks- A Study With Reference to Kadapa Corporation, Andhra Pradesh, Scheduled for Branch Offices of Select Commercial Banks

1. Name of the Bank :
2. Name of the Branch Office :
3. Date of Establishment/Commencement :
4. Total No. of staff members working in your branch :
5. Qualifications of staff members in your branch *(Put √ mark)*

   A) S.S.C b) Intermediate

   c) Graduate d) Post Graduate
6. Deposits offered in your Branch? *(Put √ mark)*

   a) Term Deposits b) Current Deposits

   c) Savings Deposits d) Any other
7. How much time it takes to consider a loan application? *(Put √ mark)*

   a) Within a Week b) Within a Month
8. If there is any delay, what are the reasons? Please Specify. *(Put √ mark)*

   a) Legal opinion

   b) approved plan

   c) Permission of municipality

   d) all
9. Please mention the basic methods you consider in sanctioning housing loan

   1. 2. 3.

10. What factors you take into account in fixing loan installments

    1. 2. 3.

12. The type of category you prefer for sanctioning of loan *(Put √ mark)*

    a) Employee b) Agriculture

    c) Business d) Others

13. Do you/your staff personally meets with the borrower for before sanctioning of loans? YES/NO

14. What type insurance is offered in your branch for house loan? *(Put √ mark)*

    a) LIC b) Postal Life

    c) Any other specify

15. How the installment amount is calculated and fixed? *(Put √ mark)*

    a) Equated b) equal

16. When payment of first installment is calculated and fixed? *(Put √ mark)*

    a) Immediately b) After _____ months

17. Interest is charged from the date of: *(Put √ mark)*

    a) loan sanction b) disbursement of loan

18. Specify the details of year wise sanctions and disbursements in your branch,

Year	*Sanctions (Rs)*	*Disbursements (Rs)*
2000-01		
2001-02		
2002-03		
2003-04		
2004-05		
2005-06		

19. The period of loan recovery for purchase/construction of new house and repairs/renovations *(Put √ mark)*

    a) 240 months b) 120 months

    c) Both

20. Are you satisfied with the recovery of loan? YES / NO

21. Specify the rate of recovery in the past five years

Year	*Rate of Recovery*
2000-01	
2001-02	
2002-03	
2003-04	
2004-05	
2005-06	

22. How many loans have been fully recovered?
    a) No.of loans within the stipulated time
    b) No.of loans after the due date
23. How many loans are outstanding even after the stipulated period?
24. Pre- Payment Schedule
25 . Any other uncovered information you would like to do add

BIBLOGRAPHY

A. BOOKS

Abrams, Charles (1964), Man's Struggle for Shelter in an Urbanizing World, Cambridge, Bombay: Vakils, Feffer Simons Pvt.Ltd.

Agarwal, A.N. (1996), Indian Economy- Problems of Development and Planning, New Delhi: Vishwa Prakashan.

Anil B. Roy Choudhary (1970), Analysis and Interpretation of Financial Statements through Financial Ratios, New Delhi: orient Longmans.

Bakshi, D., Sinha (1976), Housing Growth in India, New Delhi: Arnold Heine Mann, Published by India Pvt. India.

Basu, Ashok Rajan (1988), Urban Squatter Housing in the third World, New Delhi: Mittal Publication.

Bogan, J.J. (1957), Financial Hand Book, New York: The Ronald Press.

Braja Bandhu Padhiari and Prakash Chandra Mirsa (2004), Rural Housing Finance, New Delhi: Discovery Publishing House.

Bryce, M.D. (1960), Industrial Development, New York: McGraw Hill.

Charlu, S. (1977), Housing Economics, London: Macmillan.

Cherunilam, Francis and Heggade, Odeyan D. (1987), Housing in India, Bombay: Himalaya Publishing House.

Chowdary, A.B.R. (1970), Analysis and Interpretation is Financial Statements Statements through Financial Ratios, New Delhi: Orient Longman.

Engene, M. Learner (1971), Managerial Finance–4 systems Approach, New York: Harcourt Brace Jovanvich.

Gunnar Murdal (1970), The Challenge of World Poverty, Allen Lane the Penguin Press - London.

Helfert, E.A. (1972), Techniques of Financial Analysis, Illinois : Richard D. Irwin.

Hetal H., Patel (2001), Effectiveness of Housing and Habitat Policy, LSA-UK, Real Estate Developer, Headband: Center for Environmental Planning & Technology (CEPT).

Hingorani, N.L. and Ramanathan, A.P. (1994), Management Accounting: New Delhi: S.Chand.

Howard, B.B. and Upton, M. (1961), Introduction to Business Finance, New York: McGraw, Hill Book Company.

Huttma., E.B. (1990), Housing in Asia: Problems and Perspectives, Jaipur: Rawar Publications.

Jayam,N., and Sandhu, R.S. (1988), Housing in India: Problems, Policy and Perspective, New Delhi: B.R. Publishing Corporation.

Kennedy, R.D., and McMuller, S.Y. (1968), Financial Statements–Forms, Analysis and Interpretation, Illinois: Richard D.Irwin.

Mathur,G.C. (1977), Low Cost Housing in Developing Countries, Oxford and IBH publishing Co. Pvt. Ltd, New Delhi.

Mayo, H. (1968), Basic Finance–An Introduction to Money and Financial Management, (ed.,) New York: McGraw Hills.

Pandey, I.M. (1979), Financial Management, Bombay: Vikas Publishing House Pvt. Ltd.

Peer Smets (2007), Housing Finance for the Urban Poor: An Analysis of Self-Help Practices from Hyderabad, India, Vrije University, Delhi, Rawat.

Piyush Tiwari (1998), Housing Demand and Housing Policy in Urban India by, New Delhi: Published by Urban Studies, November.

Ramesh Babu, G. (2002), Financial Services in India, New Delhi: Concept Building Publishing Company.

Sarma (1990), Housing Finance in India, New Delhi: Sultan Chand Publication.

Singh and Sharma (2006), Housing Finance in India - A Case Study of LIC Housing Finance Limited, New Delhi: ICFAI Journal of finance Economics, Dec-4th.

Vasant Desai (2002), The Indian Financial System, Mumbai: Himalaya Publishing House, Fifth edition, May.

Venkateswarlu, U. (1998), Urbanization in India: Problems and Prospects New Delhi: New Age International Private Limited.

B. JOURNALS, MAGZINES

Aditya Jaiswal (1963), Trends in the Housing Plan Market in India, Bangalore:Asian Economic Review, Vol 40 , Issue -1.

Alpana Sivam and Sadasivam (1991), Housing and the Built Environment, Netherland: Karuppannan.

Anil Khandelwal, K. (2001), Housing Finance Increasing Competition on, Chairman, BOB Housing Finance Ltd, New Delhi: Chartered Financial Analyst, Nov.

Arimah, Ben, C. (2000), Housing Sector Performance in Global Perspective: A Cross-City Investigation, New Delhi: Published by Urban Studies, December, Vol 37, Issue 13.

Ashok Kumar, N. (1996), Securitization: Dawn of a New Era in Housing Finance, Bangolore: Southern Economist, Vol.35(4), 15th June.

Begum, Anwara (2007), Urban Housing as an Issue of Redistribution through Planning? The case of Dhak City, Dhak: social policy and administration, Black Well Publishing, August , Vol-41, No-4.

Bhattacharya, T.S. (2002), Chief General Manager of SBI's personal banking division, Hyderabad: January 5th.

Chandra Mouli, M. (1971), Housing in India-An Overview, New Delhi: Rehabilitation of Squatters in Delhi, August, Vol. XVIII, No 5.

Choyal, B.R. (1979), Financial Appraisal of State Ware-Housing Corporation: A Case Study of Rajastan Ware, Housing Corporation. A dissertation submitted for the degree of M.Phil-Department of E.A.F.M., Jaipure: University of Rajasthan, July.

Dholakia Bakul, H. (2003), Macro Economic Analysis of Housing Demand and Housing Investment in India, New Delhi: Yojana, Vol 33, Issue-4.

Das, Samantak, Housing Finance: Some Relevant Issues, New Delhi: Management Accountant, Vol 31(12), 1996.

Jasmindeep Kaur Brar and Pasricha, J.S. (2005), Housing Finance in Punjab: Sector, wise Analysis, Punjab: Mata Gujri College, Fetengarh Sahib.

Khudanpur, G.J. (1971), Housing Problems in India, Pune: Pune University.

Keshub Mahindra (2003-04), A Case Study: Housing Development Finance Corporation, Mumbai: Leading Industrialist.

Mahadeva, M. (2005), A Study of the Housing co-operatives in India with particular reference to Karnataka, Associate professor, ADRTC Bangalore.

Khan, M.Y. (2002), Housing Finance: A Perfect future, New Delhi: Chartered Financial Analyst–October.

Lakshmi Narasaiah, M. (2006), Protection Growth and Housing, UGC National Seminar, Govt. College for Men, Puttur: Aug 16th-17th.

Mahadeva, M. (2007), Housing Finance Portfolio of Scheduled Commercial Banks (SCBs)–A Trend Analysis 2000-05, National Housing Bank, May.

Mahadeva, M., and Thera Bhai (2001), Housing Finance: Can Commercial Banks Meet People Housing Finance Needs?, Bangalore: Social and Economic Change, Nagarabhavi Vol 34, No.1, Oct- Dec.

Mok, Diana (2002), Sharing the Risk of Home–Ownership: A Portfolio Approach by–New Delhi: Published by Urban studies, June, Vol 39, Issue 7.

Petter, D.F., Cardozo. Housing–Engine of Economic Growth–, Managic Director–New Delhi: AN FIN HOME Ltd.

Rao, C.S. (1998), Financing Social Housing: A Review, New Delhi: Housing Finance in India.

Rao., D.V.R. (1972), Public Sector Investments as a Tool for Larger Private Sector Participation, Some Design and Planning

Considerations, Ooty: Seminar on Economics of Housing in National Development, 5-7 May.

Samantak Das (1996), Housing Finance–Some Relevant Issues, Finance and Markets, New Delhi: Charted Accounts, December, Vol- 31, Issue 12.

Shanti, S., Tangri (1968), Urban Growth Housing and Economic Development: The Case of India, Bangalore: Asian Survey–July, Vol-8, No-7.

Shri Krishna, D. (2002), Housing Scenario in India– LICHFL, New Delhi: Urban India, Vol-7, Issue -2.

Sudhakar Reddy, K. (2006), Commercial Banks and Housing Finance in India, UGC National Seminar, Govt. College for Men, Puttur: Aug 6th -17th.

Varghese, K.V., Housing Problem in India, Pune: Gokhale Institute of Politics and Economics, April 95.

Velayudham, T.K. (1976), Debt-Equity Ratio, Mumbai: Reserve Bank of India Staff Occasional Papers, Vol. 1, No.2, December.

Housing Finance Sector will Grow 24 pc in Five Yeas (2002), Financial Daily from Hindu, Mumbai: Bureau Mumbai Wednesday, December 11th.

The Hindu (2004), Friday, Bangalore: (Edit) October 29th.

Economic Times (2006), Pune: (Edit), Friday 24th February.

Housing Development (2006): An Overview, Andhra Pradesh (Edit) Chennai: The Hindu, Aug.

Editorial (1976), New Delhi: Yojana, Dec.

NIUA Urban, Hand book 2000, New Delhi: National Institute of Urban Affairs, January 2000.

Government of Indian Draft National Housing Policy (1987), New Delhi: Ministry of Urban Development.

National Housing and Habitat Policy (2007), New Delhi: Government of India.

REPORTS AND OFFICIAL PUBLICATION

Indian Five Year Plan (2007), Complete Document, New Delhi, Academic Foundation, Vol-XII.

Icfai University, Housing Finance in India: Press report, September 20th,2007. .

The Report of Ministry of Works (1977), Housing and Supply, Government of India, New Delhi.

Reserve Bank of India Bulletin, Bombay

Annual Reports of State Bank of India, Hyderabad: (from 1999-00 to 2007-08)

Annual Reports of Andhra Bank , Hyderabad : (from 1999-00 t0 2007-08)

Annual Reports of Syndicate Bank, Manipal, Karntaka State: (from 1999-00 t0 2007-08)

Annual Reports of Indian Bank ,Madaras: (from 1999-00 t0 2007-08)

Annual Reports of Housing Development Finance Corporation, Mumbai: (from 1999-00 t0 2007-08)

Annual Reports of Housing Development Finance Corporation, New Delhi: (from 1999-00 t0 2007-08)

Annual Reports of National Housing Bank, New Delhi: (from 1999-00 t0 2005-06)

Government of India, First Five Year Plan to Eleventh Five Year Plan, New Delhi.

Government of India. Census of India, 1931 to 2001

National Housing Policy, New Delhi, 1988.

National Housing and Habitat Policy, New Delhi: 1998.

National Building Organisation, Hand Book of Housing Statistics, New Delhi:

National Housing Bank, Report on Trend and Progress of Housing in India, New Delhi: June 2000.

----Reports on trend & Progress of Housing in India, June 2001.

----Reports on trend & Progress of Housing in India, June 2002.

----Reports on trend & Progress of Housing in India, June 2003.

----Reports on trend & Progress of Housing in India, June 2004.

----Reports on trend & Progress of Housing in India, June 2005.

NEWS PAPERS

The Hindu

Eenadu (Telugu daily)

Vaartha (Telugu daily)

Business Line

Economic Times

WEB SITES

www.andf.co.uk

www.andhrabank.com

www.censusofindia.com

www.commericalbank.com

www.indianbank.co.in

www.hdfc.com

www.lichfl.com

www.lic.com

www.planningcommission.com

www.nhb.org.in

www.reservebankofindia.com

www.governmentofindia.com

www.kadapaprofile.com

www.indianbankingsystem.com

www.nho.in.org

www.hudco.org.in

www.nchf.com

www.nhhp.com.in

www.statebankofindia.co.in

www.syndicatebank.co.in